# The Twelve Days of
# Christmas

## Ideas for a More
## Meaningful Holiday Season

# The Twelve Days of Christmas

## Ideas for a More Meaningful Holiday Season

BETTY VAN ORDEN

CFI
SPRINGVILLE, UT

© 2007 Betty Van Orden

ISBN 13: 978-1-59955-050-3

Published by CFI, an imprint of Cedar Fort, Inc., 2373 W. 700 S., Springville, UT, 84663
Distributed by Cedar Fort, Inc., www.cedarfort.com

LIBRARY OF CONGRESS CATALOGING-IN-PUBLICATION DATA

Van Orden, Betty, 1943–
    The 12 Days of Christmas : Ideas for a More Meaningful Christmas /
Betty Van Orden.
        p. cm.
    ISBN 978-1-59955-050-3
    1. Christmas—Miscellanea.  I. Title.

    GT4985.V33 2007
    394.2663—dc22
                                        2007013387

Cover design by Nicole Williams
Cover design © 2007 by Lyle Mortimer
Edited by Annaliese B. Cox
Typeset by Angela Olsen

Printed in the United States of America

10  9  8  7  6  5  4  3  2  1

Printed on acid-free paper

# Dedication

To my mother, Lillian Lee LaFon,
who made every Christmas a precious memory.
I pray you are reading over my shoulder from heaven.
I love you!

# Table of Contents

# Preface

If the ideas and suggestions in this book give the reader an increased desire to express love to his or her family and to instill the act of service in their hearts during this Christmas season, then the purpose of writing this book will have been fulfilled.

# Acknowledgments

Many thanks to Cedar Fort, Inc., for believing in my ideas and allowing me the opportunity to express my heart. The experience has been incredible.

I express appreciation to my husband, Sterling, who had complete faith in me that this book could be written. His love and his encouragement brought this book to fruition. I love you, Sterling.

This book would never have had a purpose without the six precious gifts I have in my life and whom I cherish and love with all my heart—our beautiful children, Kaye, Heather, Stephanie, Jason, Julie, and Jon David. I thank God daily for the privilege and honor of being your mother. And thank you to Joe, Theron, Kelly, and Jill, who are the perfect mates for our children. You are each an amazing gift in my life.

To our grandchildren; Justin, Taylor, Cameron, Allison, Joseph, Nicholas, Vincent, Ethan, Jessica, Brianne, Rachel, Brooke, Nathan, Adam, Ashley, Bowen, Austin, Brynlee, Ellie, and Chloe—indeed, you make my heart sing! You have made this experience so much fun! Thank you for loving me!

To my friends and colleagues at the Conference Center, thank you for your confidence in me. To Joyce Goodrich and Barbara Salisbury, thank you for the many hours you spent with me along the way. I'm blessed to have you in my life. To Karla Erickson, Jackie Katuschenko, Linda Elkins, Harriett Sharpe, and Arlene Zucker—my cheering squad! God truly blessed me with wonderful friends.

And to my brother, Eddie, thanks for the cherished memories. I miss your phone calls . . . and you!

# Introduction

*"Oh, parents, we would plead, give good and happy memories to your children—not pampering or overindulging, not satisfying everything they take a fancy to—but memories of love, encouragement, of peace and harmony and happiness at home—memories that will bless and lift their lives wherever they are, always and forever."*

—L. Tom Perry,
*The Improvement Era*, Dec. 1970

It happened before we knew it. Our little ones were grown up all too soon. It was such a short season to have our children in our home. And then they were off to their separate colleges, missions, and marriages. We thought our responsibilities with our six children were pretty much completed. Oh . . . how wrong we were! Soon they began filling our lives with these amazing little creatures we call grandchildren. Could there be anything more perfect to grace our lives than grandchildren? They bring joy and inspiration along with the desire to make our lives even more meaningful. We realize now that our never-ending mission on this earth is to love and to teach those entrusted to our care. Through the years I have become more aware of the influence for good that we, as parents, can have over our children and grandchildren, as well as recognizing and encouraging the good that already exists within them.

Perhaps this is where my desire to change Christmas traditions in our home began. I knew that if I wanted a change to take place, then it had to begin with me. As Ghandi said, "We must become the change we wish to see in the world." This change wasn't going to happen all by itself! I had a yearning—no, it was more than a yearning: my heart was crying out within me—to "make a difference"! I wanted to see our family, our children and grandchildren, celebrating the birth of the Savior with more meaning in their hearts and with more action in their lives. I wanted to help provide a Christmas for our family that would touch their hearts each day.

These feelings of making Christmas all it could and should be within our family were consuming me. I knew there was an answer—I just needed to find it! Making this a matter of prayer, I went daily to my Heavenly Father and told him of my concern for our family and my desire to make a change. God's grace goes beyond the effects of the Atonement. His hand moves in our behalf on many occasions in our lives. Through his love we are able to accomplish many things that we otherwise would not be able to do on our own. I have great faith that I can trust my Heavenly Father to always hear and answer my prayers. These answers had come to me many times throughout my life, and I knew that an answer would come again.

Sometimes we grandparents forget we have a major leadership role in our families and that we can impact the lives of those we love. We get wrapped up in our busy lives and often neglect to ponder the areas where we can truly make a difference.

*"Listening is an essential part of praying. Answers from the Lord come quietly, ever so quietly. In fact, few hear His answers audibly with their ears. We must be listening so carefully or we will never recognize them. Most answers from the Lord are felt in our heart as a warm comfortable expression, or they may come as thoughts to our mind. They come to those who are prepared and who are patient."*

—H. BURKE PETERSON,
*The Improvement Era,* OCT. 1974

# Chapter One

*How the Change Began*

*"Go forward in life with a twinkle in your eye and a smile on your face, but with great and strong purpose in your heart."*

—Gordon B. Hinckley,
*Ensign*, May 2001

My brother, Eddie, passed away several months before Christmas. The Christmas season had always been Eddie's favorite time of the year. I remember his phone calls to me in late November. "Betty," he'd say, "I'm finishing up the outside decorations and it's looking great!" His house was decorated from top to bottom, with lights strewn on the outside of the house, candles in the windows, and always, always a nativity scene in the front yard.

I loved those phone calls and could hardly wait to hear the excitement in his voice as he carefully described the scene in such detail that I could easily picture it in my mind. We were never fortunate to live close to one another, but our phone calls kept us close in heart. We often met at Mom and Dad's for the holidays when our children were younger, but as they grew up we knew it was only right that they celebrate Christmas in their own homes. Beautiful memories were made both in the home of their grandparents and in our own homes.

I sat pondering the memories and wondering why Eddie had to leave us at such a young age. Hey, fifty-nine sounds pretty young the older you get! This would be a different holiday for me; my mother had passed away six years earlier, and now my brother, too, was gone. I told myself that I would keep both of their memories alive forever and that this Christmas would be dedicated to them. I would sincerely try to make it a special holiday in every way.

Have you ever felt that you were spending money and time during the holidays but wondered if any of it was really spent the way it should be? That was the way I felt on this particular day.

My thoughts went back to the Christmas Day a few years before when our grandchildren arrived to open our gifts to them. They ran down the stairs to the family room, grabbed their gifts, quickly opened them while throwing wrapping paper all over the room, yelled a quick "thank you," and off they went. This all happened before their parents joined them, so the parents had no inkling of the many hours that we had spent making sure the gifts were beautifully wrapped, nor did they know which gift was for which child! There was definitely something wrong with this, and I knew it. Christmas just wasn't what it used to be.

I began to open my heart to prayer, and suddenly I was aware of how much I wanted to fulfill my desire. I pleaded with my Heavenly Father, "Is there something I can do to bring more meaning to Christmas in our home? If so, how can I go about it?" There had to be an answer because my Heavenly Father knew my desire came through my love for my family. The gifts were always fun, but they *had* to have more meaning.

Sitting by the fireplace one evening, I was reminded of someone who had presented the 12 Days of Christmas to a friend, each day delivering a special gift. What a fun idea. Could I do this for our family? They would be terribly excited knowing a gift was coming to them daily; but how could I make the gifts special? I didn't want to shop for gifts that had no purpose or meaning.

Later that evening I shared my thoughts with my husband, Sterling. At first he thought I was biting off more than I could chew (I've been known to do that on many occasions). But the more we talked, the more excited we became, until we finally knew that this was something we wanted to do—if we could make it fit the needs of our family. We tossed ideas back and forth, and I was thrilled with the excitement Sterling showed. I knew already that this was going to be an incredible Christmas, and I could hardly wait to put our plans into action. Ideas began to flood my mind and heart. I ran to the computer and began typing as fast as my fingers would go. I spent many hours pondering and praying about the 12 Days of Christmas for our family.

Each day I presented new ideas to Sterling. He shared in my excitement but was still working full time, so I made most of the preparations. We decided that a yearly theme would be the focus for our Christmas holiday. We would decide what we felt was most important for our family to focus on and plan our gifts around that theme.

It is amazing what the mind can come up with when the heart is involved. Let me be clear in saying that what felt good and right for me and my family may not be what is most important for your family—you may need to adjust these ideas so they can work for you. You will understand this better as we go along.

# Chapter Two

## *Family*

*There is no ideal Christmas; only the one Christmas you decide to make as a reflection of your values, desires, affections, traditions.*

—Bill McKibben

We chose "Family" as the theme for the first year, and we especially wanted to stress the importance of families being eternal. Our family is fortunate to live close to one another, and we consider that a great blessing. This was especially helpful in planning the 12 Days of Christmas. If your family lives out of town and you will need to mail your gifts you will find that most of my ideas can be adjusted for easy mailing.

Sterling and I agreed to keep our 12 Days of Christmas a secret so it could be a wonderful surprise for the children. The only clue they would have was that on the fourteenth day of December, their dad and I would visit each of their homes. Oh, can you imagine the excitement going on within our family! Each person had his own idea of what was going to happen.

We kept everything locked in our extra bedroom so no one could sneak a peak and ruin our surprise. We purchased large, red plastic containers with green tops for each family in which we placed the completed gifts, all wrapped and numbered. We filled each container with twelve gifts to be delivered on December 14th to each home so that one gift could be taken from the container daily.

We included a cover letter explaining to the family exactly what we were doing and what they were to do. Let me share with you our first cover letter, printed on Christmassy paper, placed in a plastic sleeve, and taped to the outside of the plastic container so it would be read first:

To our precious children and grandchildren,

This year we want to do something a little different for you and your family. We want to celebrate . . . *the 12 Days of Christmas!*

Each morning you can take out one gift, starting with Day #1 and going through to Day #12. Each day's gift will be marked on the outside so you will know which gift to open. Inside is a message explaining the gift.

We believe in eternal families, and we need to work toward that goal. Therefore, our theme for this year will be "Family." we want to stress that each gift be shared together as a family. You will be able to make wonderful memories together as a family that you will cherish forever as you take part in this new adventure.

We have had such fun preparing these special gifts for you and hope you will feel the love in each one.

May our Heavenly Father be with you as you celebrate the birth of his Son, Jesus Christ. Please express your love to one another at this special time of the year as our Savior would have us do. Grandchildren, this is a great time to be a helper to Mom and Dad and show your love for them. This is what makes families special—we help and love one another.

We love each one of you with all our hearts and are especially thankful that you are a part of our family. We look forward to being with you during this special Christmas holiday and sharing our love as a family. Merry Christmas!

—*Mom and Dad*
(NeNa and PaPa)

On the inside of each package, we placed a note telling about the gift. We put it on the inside so they couldn't sneak and read the messages before the appointed day. Most of the gifts were quite simple and easy to prepare. Some years we had more time, so we were able to make the gifts a little more special. Each gift was prepared and given with more love than our children and grandchildren could ever have imagined. It has been an exciting challenge thinking of ideas that would be both meaningful and fun and still go along with our theme for the year in some way. These were our choices of gifts the first year, along with the comments on the tag attached to each gift.

On the FIRST Day of

# Christmas

*We bring to you with love . . .*

Homemade Fudge! To be enjoyed as you gather 'round the Christmas tree as a family. Spend time together talking about your plans for the holidays and how you can make this Christmas extra special for your family. Remember . . . we love you!

*Our children and grandchildren love my homemade fudge and request it every year—so they always get fudge in a pretty Christmas tin on the first day so it will be fresh! See page 66 for the recipe.*

On the SECOND Day of

# Christmas

*We bring to you with love . . .*

Gift Certificates for Milk Shakes! We all love a special treat, so here are some gift certificates for your favorite milk shake. Sometime today or tonight we hope you will take time to enjoy your favorite milk shake together as a family. We will be thinking of you and picturing your happy faces!

*Naturally, any food item can be chosen from any restaurant.*

On the THIRD Day of

*Christmas*

*We bring to you with love . . .*

A New DVD and a Box of Cookie Mix! Be sure you bake these cookies together before you begin the movie. Yummy! Nothing beats a good movie, freshly baked cookies, and being with those you love. Remember, you are each surrounded with love.

*We have given a Christmas DVD each year, so the families are beginning to get a nice collection of Christmas movies.*

On the FOURTH Day of

# Christmas

*We bring to you with love . . .*

Homemade Lollipops! These are straight from NeNa's kitchen! Friends are so important in our lives, and during this special time of the year we want to tell them so. Take a lollipop for you and one for your best friend! Tell them what a great friend they are to you. Each one of you is an amazing friend!

*We have included the homemade lollipops each year. I added an additional message the next year that said: "Yes, once again we are giving these lollipops to you to share with your best friend—is it the same person this year or do you have a new best friend? It is wonderful to make new friends, but never forget the ones you have made in the past. Friends are beautiful treasures in our lives."*

You may remember these words: "Make new friends but keep the old; one is silver and the other gold." We want this to be the feeling within their hearts. Our grandson, Nicholas, commented that he needed a lot more than one extra lollipop because he had so many friends! He requested that we give him a lot more next year. This is exactly what we were hoping would happen. We want our grandchildren to grasp the meaning and value of friendship.

## Homemade Lollipops

1 cup sugar
½ cup water
⅓ cup white corn syrup
1 tsp. flavoring
food coloring (paste)

Combine sugar, water, and corn syrup in small saucepan. Cook on medium-high heat until mixture reaches 300 degrees. Remove and let cool to 275 degrees. Add flavoring and food coloring. Stir until blended. Pour into greased molds. Allow to cool until candy is set.

❋ *Grease inside of molds with non-stick spray. Place molds on lightly greased flat surface—a marble slab or cookie sheets works great.*

You should be able to find lollipop molds and flavorings at any local craft or confectionery store. The above recipe makes about 20 lollipops. You can find fun Christmas molds in all sorts of shapes: snowmen, Santas, stars, angels, trees, gingerbread men, and lots of others. There are many flavorings to choose from as well; some of our favorites have been watermelon, wild cherry, peppermint, strawberry, cotton candy, orange, and blueberry.

You'll love how beautiful they look when you get them finished. Try adding some candy eyes to Santas, gingerbread men, snowmen, and angels. Also, there are small plastic bags made just for lollipops so you'll want to use those and secure them with tape. Add some colorful ribbon, if you like. If homemade isn't for you, stores are full of holiday lollipops.

On the FIFTH Day of

# Christmas

*We bring to you with love . . .*

**Five Dollars for a Service Project!** You may use the money however you choose—buy ingredients to make cookies or candy, or you might choose to purchase a Christmas plant for someone special. Each family member might want to contribute to this amount so you can do even more service. Choose your service project together as a family. This is a great way to begin your Christmas service, and what better way is there to celebrate the birth of Christ than by remembering those in need? As we get together for our family Christmas dinner, please share your service project with our family. Make this a project of love.

*Each year we have included a service project. Service in any form is beautiful, whether it is service to our families, friends, or those whom we meet along life's path. We should love them and show this love through our actions. Our service pales in comparison to the service shown by the Master teacher.*

On the SIXTH Day of

# Christmas

*We bring to you with love . . .*

**Ornaments for Your Memory Tree!** These bread dough ornaments we are giving you were made years ago when our children were young. They hung on our Christmas tree for many years, and now some of them hang on our memory tree. This year we want to share them with you as you begin your own memory tree. It can be a small tree until you accumulate more memories over the years. It will become one of your most cherished decorations! Take a few minutes tonight and talk about the decorations on your tree and some of your favorite Christmas memories.

*A memory tree is a tree that hangs full of ornaments we have accumulated through the years beginning when our children were in kindergarten. What do you do with the cute little ornaments your children bring home and you want to hold on to forever? We found that the memory tree was our answer. Our tree holds memories of everything—even an ornament from my Christmas tree when I was a little girl.*

One year we purchased ball ornaments with little recorders in them. Sterling and I recorded messages to each family. The grandchildren enjoyed pushing the button and listening to NeNa and PaPa talk to them. You can find these message recorders at most stores that sell Christmas ornaments.

Another year we included an ornament from the Winter Olympics held in Utah. Another year was an ornament from a vacation we shared together. Let your imagination run wild, and you'll have a great time with this one.

When each of our children married, we placed one of their wedding pictures in a small frame, inscribed with the date of their wedding, and gave it to them the next Christmas for their memory tree. The same can be done with each birth of a child, blessing, baptism, mission, and so forth. Oh, and don't forget their pets! They will love having an ornament with a picture of their pet on it. Any events that took place during the year or an event from the past is always special. Our memory tree hangs full of cherished memories!

## Bread Dough Ornaments

2 cups flour

½ cup salt

¾ cup *cold* water

Mix together well. Roll out to about ¼-inch thick on a lightly floured board. Dip cookie cutters in flour before using. *Be sure* to put a small hole in the top of each ornament before baking that you can fit a string or ribbon through to hang it by. Bake at 250 degrees for 3 to 4 hours. Let cool completely; then paint with acrylic paints. When the paint has dried completely, spray with a hi-gloss spray for protection. Any fun cookie cutter can be used for the holiday. I have used Santas, snowmen, Christmas trees, bells, and angels. Raggedy Ann and Andy cutters are especially adorable; I used a garlic press to make the hair so they were just perfect.

On the SEVENTH Day of

*Christmas*

*We bring to you with love . . .*

Flavored Popcorn! This is always a fun treat, and we hope you will enjoy the different flavors. Tonight we want you to sit together as a family and talk about how much you are loved by your parents or children, your brothers and sisters, your friends, your grandparents, and, most important, how much you are loved by your Heavenly Father. We need to show love to others at Christmas time and all during the year. Hugs and kisses are important. Remember how much NeNa and PaPa love you!

*You could substitute a bag of chocolate Hugs or Kisses or microwavable popcorn if you are sending your gifts by mail. Another idea is homemade popcorn balls wrapped in green or red cellophane and tied with ribbon. Since our families live close by, we gave them Christmas tins filled with different flavors of popcorn.*

## Popcorn Balls

½ cup butter
1 cup sugar
½ cup white corn syrup
¼ teaspoon salt

Combine all ingredients and bring to a boil; boil for 1 minute.
Pour over 8 to 9 cups popped corn and stir. Butter your hands
and shape into popcorn balls.

## Gelatin Popcorn Balls

1 cup light corn syrup
½ cup sugar
1 small pkg. gelatin (any flavor)

Bring to a boil and pour over 8 to 9 cups popped corn. Butter
hands and shape into balls. Choose a seasonal color of gelatin.

On the EIGHTH Day of

# Christmas

*We bring to you with love . . .*

## A Christmas Storybook and Candy Canes!

Tonight we want you to enjoy a yummy candy cane while you quietly listen to Mom or Dad read you this beautiful Christmas book. Perhaps you will want to sit around the Christmas tree. Be sure to do this as a family. Have fun! We love you.

*You could include the story on the following page with your candy canes.*

# Story of the Candy Cane

There were once two villages in a far-off land. One was in a valley and one was on a mountain top. The folks in the mountain village wanted to give each person in the valley village a gift of love at Christmas. The people in the valley were having difficult times, but those in the mountain village were doing well.

Sometimes when we are on a mountain top, we can help those who are going through a valley in their lives. That is what these mountain folks wanted to do as well. So, the townspeople formed a committee to see if they could think of something special to give. Money was limited, and each gift had to be of equal value to each person. After much time, discussion, and consideration, a decision was finally reached.

An elderly gentleman who had loved Jesus for many years and who was well respected and loved came up with the idea of a candy cane. Now, you are thinking, what is so special about a candy cane, and how can it ever be tied in with Christmas? Here is how and why . . .

❉ The candy cane is in the shape of a shepherd's staff. Jesus is our shepherd and we are his flock. A sheep follows his own shepherd, knows his voice, and trusts him—he knows he is totally safe with him. A sheep will follow no other shepherd but his own. This is how we should be with Jesus if we truly follow him.

❉ Upside down, the cane is a J—the first letter of Jesus' name.

❉ The wide red stripes represent the blood he shed on the cross for each one of us so that through him we can have eternal life. He redeems us and cleanses us with his blood, which is the only thing that can wash away our sins.

❉ The white stripes represent the sinlessness and purity of our Lord. He is the only human being that ever lived on this earth who never committed a single sin. Even though he was tempted, just as we are, he never sinned.

❉ The narrow red stripe symbolizes that by his own stripes, or wounds, we are healed. Before the crucifixion, Jesus was beaten, a crown of thorns was placed on his head, and his back was raw from being whipped. We are healed by those wounds. He bore our sorrows, and by his stripes we are healed.

❋ The flavoring in the candy cane is peppermint, which is similar to hyssop. Hyssop is part of the mint family and was used in the Old Testament for purification and sacrifice.

❋ When we break our candy cane, it reminds us that Jesus' body was broken for us. When we take the sacrament, this is our reminder of what he did for us.

—ANONYMOUS

On the NINTH Day of

# Christmas

*We bring to you with love . . .*

A Christmas Coloring Book, Crayons, and a New Game! Coloring pictures and playing games can be such fun when you do this together as a family. You will make wonderful memories. Take some time today to color some pictures with the children and play your new game. The children will love this and so will you. We'll be thinking of you.

*This idea is one that would be easy to mail. Be sure to add the date, the name of the little artist, and the child's age when the page is completed. These make wonderful keepsakes for parents and grand-parents!*

On the TENTH Day of

*Christmas*

*We bring to you with love . . .*

White Chocolate Peppermint Bark! Yes, today you will enjoy some homemade peppermint bark that you love so much. Perhaps you can eat it while sitting around your Christmas tree this evening. Remember the fun we have had making this in the past. We cherish our memories of time spent with each one of you.

*Follow the scrumptious family recipe on the following page.*

# White Chocolate Peppermint Bark

10 regular size candy canes
2 lbs. white chocolate

Line a cookie sheet with wax paper or parchment paper. Unwrap candy canes and place them in a heavy-duty plastic bag. Using a rolling pin, crush the candy canes into small pieces. Set aside. In a double boiler, melt white chocolate. Be careful not to scorch the chocolate—white chocolate will scorch quickly. Stir in most of the crushed candy canes, reserving some to sprinkle on top. Pour chocolate mixture into prepared cookie sheet, spreading into an even layer. Sprinkle chunks of candy cane on top. Refrigerate for about 20 minutes or until set. Remove bark from parchment paper and break into chunks by hand. Store in a tightly covered container.

*This is great to give as gifts when placed in a glass container or cellophane wrap so the colors can show through. Also consider this recipe when making gifts that have to be mailed.*

On the ELEVENTH Day of

Christmas

We bring to you with love . . .

## Hot Chocolate Mix and Christmas Mugs!

Today is Christmas Eve, and we are excited because we will get to share this special day with you. How fun to be together as we wait for Santa to arrive! Let's share a cup of cocoa tonight before we go to bed, okay? We have included lots of hot chocolate mix so you can make several cups of cocoa throughout the day. We hope you have had fun looking forward to your special treat each day.

*Follow the recipe for hot chocolate mix on the following page or buy your favorite kind of mix at the store. There are all kinds of cozy flavors to choose from.*

# Hot Chocolate Mix

1½ cups sugar
1 cup powdered non-dairy creamer
1 cup dry powdered milk
¾ cup unsweetened cocoa powder

Mix together and store in air-tight container. When ready to serve, put 2 to 3 tablespoons of powder in a mug. Fill with hot water and mix well.

*Don't forget to add some marshmallows on top!*

On the TWELFTH Day of

*Christmas*

*We bring to you with love . . .*

A Gift Certificate for a Family Portrait! Since our theme this year for the 12 Days of Christmas has been families, we thought it would be a great idea to have a new family picture taken. We hope you will find a special place to put your new picture so that it can be enjoyed by everyone who visits your home. Be sure to smile! We love you. Oh, and remember to use your storage container for packing away your Christmas decorations.

*This is a great gift because you get the gift as well!*

# Chapter Three

## *Letter to Parents*

*"Grandparents are like a piece of string—handy to have around and easily wrapped around the fingers of their grandchildren.*

—Author Unknown

Little did Sterling and I know that one of the greatest joys we would ever receive came in the form of a letter that was presented to us on Christmas morning as all our children and grandchildren gathered at our home. They opened their gift for the 12th Day of Christmas and expressed their delight in having a coupon for a new family portrait. Then our eldest daughter, Kaye, asked everyone in the room to quietly listen as I read aloud a letter from the children of the thoughts and reactions they had accumulated while enjoying the 12 Days of Christmas. Oh, how unfair of them to have me read it aloud! I could hardly speak through the tears, but somehow I managed to read what is now one of our most precious keepsakes, one that we will treasure forever. Let me share with you some of what that letter said:

### The 12 Days of Love

We, as your children and grandchildren, can never fully repay you for the hours you must have spent in putting together this wonderful Christmas for us and our families. We have put together these thoughts and reactions for you to read and keep as a reminder that, yes, all of your time and efforts were very much appreciated.

Mom and Dad, we love you very much. You have reminded us of the importance of showing love to our Savior, and for this we are eternally grateful. Read on, and remember you are loved by all of your children.

✳ ✳ ✳

Our family has had so much fun being a part of the 12 Days of Christmas. The first day began with a bang. The kids woke up at 6:30 that morning so excited to open the first present. So at 6:40, Joey and I were hearing the sounds of our four little boys chiming, "Mommy, can we have fudge for breakfast?" No wonder they were bouncing off the walls all day!

As we sat around the Christmas tree, we were amazed that the kids could sit so calmly as we read the stories you gave us, discussed what service project we could do together, and talked about the true meaning of Christmas. Every day the kids woke up so excited to open that day's present. We enjoyed the popcorn; it became a lovely "ground cover" for the family room. The children kept busy on an extremely chaotic Saturday by coloring and playing games together. How perfect to spend a Sunday evening baking cookies and watching a video about the Savior. Choosing a friend to give the special lollipops to was wonderful.

This brings us to what we have learned from the 12 Days of Christmas: it's when one child says, "Mommy, I know what Christmas is really about . . . it's about helping others and loving Jesus. I love Jesus, Mommy." With all the hard work both of you have put into this, if only one child realizes what the true meaning of Christmas really is, then it was absolutely worth it. I found out the true meaning of Christmas by watching you, Mom and Dad, as I grew up. You taught me about true sacrifice for the ones you loved by emulating the Savior's example. And now, once again, you've been an example through the love and sacrifice you've put into the 12 Days of Christmas. Thank you for loving our kids and us so much. Merry Christmas!

—HEATHER, AGE 33

✳ ✳ ✳

It has been so much fun spending time with my siblings as we tried to figure out the Christmas surprise! We reflected upon the memories of Christmas as children growing up in our home. We all know we are loved when two people put so much time and thought into a Christmas surprise. The fudge was honestly the best I have ever eaten! I was excited to get the box of candy canes. Sounds silly, huh? I love having a couple of candy canes every year. I was recently talking to Mom about how I wanted to do something special for someone this Christmas. Thank you, Mom and Dad, for helping Kelly and me share with others at this time of the year.

—JASON, AGE 27

\* \* \*

We have spent time talking about what an awesome gift this has been and how it helps bring the true spirit of Christmas into our home. We want to thank you for doing this. It is truly amazing! Instead of thinking of things we may have told you we wanted for Christmas, you gave us gifts of things that have true meaning in our lives. We are using our service money to serve some elderly widows in our community. We are making cookies and will deliver them on December 20th. I can hardly wait to see their faces! They will be just as excited that they have someone to visit them during the holidays as they will be to get the cookies. We will take Bowen with us, and I'm sure they will love having a little one-year-old visit them. The true meaning of Christmas is not decorating your home or buying gifts. It is to remember Christ and his gift to us. Christ served others and we as a family thought it was great that Mom and Dad believe in service so much that they gave us money to encourage us to serve others. We will make it a family tradition each year.

—JULIE, AGE 24

\* \* \*

The funniest thing about our box with the 12 Days of Christmas presents is that Theron was just as excited as the kids were! That night, after you delivered the box, I asked Theron to put it in the family room. He didn't like that idea because it was too far from his bed in the morning. So, the box is right next to our bed—on his side. It was fun to share with my daughters the memories I had of coming home from school and smelling different flavors of lollipops. I let them know that I helped put the lollipops in bags and tape them. I hope to someday share this tradition with my girls. It was fun for them to decide with which friends they would share the lollipops. Day 5 had such beautiful meaning for our family. I shared my idea of what we could do for our service project, and the girls and Theron were thrilled. We will share this with you on Christmas Day.

—STEPHANIE, AGE 30

\* \* \*

It was fun seeing Dad so excited. He was full of love the day you came to deliver the Christmas box to our home. It was great seeing that he had also helped. Usually Mom does all the shopping, and Dad will just okay it. But this time both Mom and Dad put a lot of time and effort together, making it a Christmas to remember. Taylor and Justin were just as excited each morning as their younger siblings, Cameron and Allison. We will never forget this. I'm sure we will all use this idea for our children in years to come. Thank you.

—KAYE, AGE 35

❄ ❄ ❄

This is the last year Jill and I will be alone for Christmas since our baby will be arriving in February. We have spent a lot of time planning how we want to celebrate Christmas in our home. Thank you for starting a collection of Christmas DVDs for us along with the beautiful Christmas book. Jill is very excited about the memory tree and can hardly wait to get more ornaments for ours. What a great idea for us as we begin our little family and make memories together. This has been an incredible experience with the 12 Days of Christmas, and we will never forget it.

—JON DAVID, AGE 22

❄ ❄ ❄

No matter what Day 12 brings, we know it comes wrapped in love from our parents. We love you both. You called it the 12 Days of Christmas—we called it the 12 Days of Love.

—*Your Children*

With a reception like that, how could we not want to experience these feelings again? I share this to show how deeply your own family can be touched with the simple things you do for them.

We keep our eyes and ears open all year for meaningful ideas and gifts. Each family is different, so you will need to adapt these ideas to fit your family. Even if my ideas aren't exactly what you want for your family, they can get you thinking so you can come up with something even better for your family.

We have continued using some of the ideas we used that first year, and now the children and grandchildren look forward to a new Christmas or Disney DVD to add to their collection and a new Christmas storybook and game they can share together as a family. Of course, our goal is to provide lots of things they can do together.

# Chapter Four

*Memories with Love*

*At Christmas, all roads lead home.*

—Marjorie Holmes

Christmas 2002 was another wonderful year. We decided on a theme that we felt sure would touch the hearts of our children: "Memories with Love." Recalling good memories always sets a sweet tone in our homes.

On the FIRST Day of

# Christmas

*We bring to you with love . . .*

A Christmas Quilt! Today you are receiving a warm quilt to snuggle under as you share time together during the holidays. It has been made with hours of love just for your special family. Oh, how we love you!

*While babysitting our four grandsons, I fell down the stairs. I was not able to get around very well for a while after that. I went to therapy, but it took a long time for my leg to heal. I was down but not out, so I decided to make good use of my time. Sterling set up the sewing machine each morning, and I sewed all day with one leg wrapped in a heating pad and elevated on a chair while the other leg was used on the pedal. I was quite a sight to see!*

This was the year I made a queen-size rag quilt for each family—six of them. We referred to it as their Christmas quilts, and I found a wonderful poem to go along with each one. Use this idea if you have some extra time on your hands during the year, but get an early start if you have a large family. It's a great winter project.

## Ideas for a Rag Quilt

✳ Choose a fabric that suits each family receiving a quilt. I have found that cotton, flannel, and denim will give the best "rag" look. Fleece is pretty but doesn't fray as nicely.

✳ Decide what size you want the quilt to be. Cut out 96 (6-inch) squares of different colors. I used flannels with Christmas patterns that were great for the season.

✳ Then cut 48 (4-inch) squares of quilt batting. You don't want the batting to show after the quilt has been made "ragged," so it has to be cut smaller than the fabric squares. I like a fluffier quilt, so I use a thicker batting, but some prefer the rag quilt to be thinner. It's a matter of choice. You can adjust the number of squares you will need according to the size you want your quilt to be as well.

✳ Layer the batting between 2 squares of fabric and sew each square from corner to corner, making an *X* to secure the batting. You should have 48, 3-layered squares with an *X* on each. You are now ready to lay the squares out in the pattern you have chosen.

✳ If you like a set pattern, use the familiar ABC pattern. Pin the squares together and sew down the seam, using a 1-inch seam allowance on each square. Add on squares until you reach the desired size of your quilt; I use 8 squares. Remember to keep your pattern in order.

✳ Now sew the rows of 8 squares together using the 1-inch seam allowance. Continue sewing each row together until you have completed your quilt. You should end up with 6 rows of 8 squares each.

❄Sew a 1-inch seam all the way around the outside of your quilt. Clip each side of every square. The smaller the clipping, the better your quilt will rag.

This is a very rewarding project, but keep in mind that there are many alternatives to this: tie a quilt, make a fleece quilt, or purchase a quilt already made. That's the fun of it. You can do whatever fits into your schedule.

The children have cherished these quilts and often comment that they are sure their quilt was the prettiest of all! This is the poem we used with our Christmas quilts. (You'll want to insert your grandchildren's names in place of these.)

## Christmas Quilt Magic

The date today is the fourteenth of December.
It's time to make memories we will long remember,
So Mom and Dad this very night
In the Christmas quilt will wrap up tight.
The next night will be Jessica's turn;
The oldest child this spot does earn.

The third night the quilt on Brianne's bed will be,
And she'll dream of treasures 'neath the tree.
Then Rachel and Brooke their turn will take
To have visions of Christmas before they awake.
After Nathan, the youngest, has felt Christmas wonder,
The cycle repeats, with more Christmas-quilt slumber.
The Christmas quilt magic will come to full flower
When the family all gathers for a Christmas Eve hour.
They'll leave cookies and milk for old Santa to eat,
And he'll rest under the quilt after his holiday treat.

On the SECOND Day of

# Christmas

*We bring to you with love . . .*

**Christmas Pillowcases!** This year each member of your family is receiving his or her own Christmas pillowcase. Lay your head on the pillowcase each night and enjoy sweet dreams of Christmas. We are dreaming of wonderful Christmas surprises for you.

*While a dear friend was visiting me, we enjoyed spending time choosing Christmas fabric for the pillowcases and sewing together. It was a wonderful memory for us to share as we prepared fun pillowcases for our grandchildren. The grandchildren loved having a special Christmas pillowcase all their own. I was fortunate to find a poem that fit perfectly, and I have included it on the following page.*

# Merry Christmas!

December fourteenth starts a magical time,
With all sorts of colors, stories, and rhyme.
Sugar plums and fairies will dance in your head
If you lay this pillowcase on top of your bed.
The reason it is special as you will soon see
Is 'cause it's been dusted with "Christmas fantasy."
Visions of candy canes, Santa, and treasures
Will fill your dreams with sweetness and pleasures.
When the time comes that it needs to be washed,
Do it so quickly that no magic is lost!

—ANONYMOUS

The moms in our families reported that the pillowcases were a huge hit, and they could hardly get the children to part with them long enough to have them washed.

## Standard Size Pillowcases

❋Cut 27 inches of Christmas fabric (45 inches wide).

❋Cut 9 inches of contrast print, fold to 4½ inches wide, and press.

❋Cut 4-inch piece of either red or green broadcloth, fold to 2 inches wide, and press.

❋Layer 27-inch piece, then 2-inch piece, and finally 4½-inch piece.

❋Sew through all three layers. This forms the casing and trim (2-inch piece).

❋Finally, sew end across and down one side.

On the THIRD Day of

# Christmas

*We bring to you with love . . .*

A Family Collage! Here are some special pictures of our extended family that we have arranged in this framed collage for you. We have included some yummy Christmas candy for the grandchildren.

*We enclosed a special message with the collage. It is included in the following page.*

Our dear children,

These are pictures of your great-grandparents, your grandparents, your parents, your siblings, and you. What fun we had
finding these pictures and preparing this collage for you! Find a
special place in your home where this can hang and be seen by
your children each day. They will know the faces of their ancestors
and feel a connection with them even though they weren't able
to meet them on this earth. This is a special gift for the parents,
so we have also included a treat for the children . . . a bag of
Christmas candy. Merry Christmas! We love you.

We actually filled the collage with pictures of our grandparents, our
parents, and Sterling and me at our wedding and our high school graduations. We also included pictures of each of our children at their weddings
and high school graduations. When we finished, it was fun to see each
of us at approximately the same age. This has helped the grandchildren
become familiar with their heritage.

On the FOURTH Day of

# Christmas

*We bring to you with love . . .*

**Six Jars of NeNa Butter!** We know how much you love NeNa Butter, so we wanted to surprise you with some to eat during the holidays. This will bring lots of "sweet" memories of your sweet grandmother, my mother. She loved surprising us with her NeNa Butter too.

*When I was a young girl, my mother would make homemade apple butter. It would fill the house with the aroma of cinnamon and apples. I treasure the memory of Mother baking a pan of delicious homemade biscuits, putting out a jar of her apple butter, and telling us to eat all we wanted. Eddie and I could hardly wait to have such a yummy treat.*

As the years passed and I married and had children of my own, I often thought that I should make some homemade apple butter. Then, one Christmas Mother surprised our family with a dozen jars of her homemade specialty. She had purchased decorative jars and tied colorful ribbons around the top. Mother had a wonderful gift of making simple things look beautiful. Our children absolutely loved the treat but couldn't remember what it was called, so they began calling it "NeNa Butter" (they called my mother NeNa also), and the name stuck.

I have learned to make "NeNa Butter," and now our grandchildren love it just as much as their parents do. Sterling and I spent several days making the apple butter, putting it into pretty little jars, and, yes, tying ribbons around the top. One convenient thing about making apple butter or jelly of any kind is that it can be made early and hidden away until Christmas.

## NeNa Butter (Apple Butter)

9 cups applesauce

5 cups sugar

2 Tbsp. vinegar

1 medium size pkg. Cinnamon Red-Hot candy

1 drop cinnamon oil

I have found that using a good brand of applesauce makes the apple butter much thicker, so you don't have to cook it quite as long. Place all ingredients into a slow cooker and cook on low heat for about 4 hours. You'll know when it's done because the applesauce will have thickened. Pour into prepared jars as you would for any jam or jelly.

On the FIFTH Day of

# Christmas

*We bring to you with love . . .*

A Family Cookbook! Here are many of the recipes you have loved and wanted for a long time. They have been made into a family cookbook for you to use and enjoy. Make good memories together cooking up these recipes.

*My cousin Pat asked everyone in our family to send her our favorite recipes, and she compiled them into a family cookbook. It turned out great, and I was proud to include it in the 12 Days of Christmas. It was a big hit. Who doesn't like new recipes—especially when they are from people you know and love? This fit our theme beautifully.*

On the SIXTH Day of

# Christmas

*We bring to you with love . . .*

Our Love Story! We have a unique and beautiful love story to share with you. You've heard this story many times over the years, but we want to make sure our grandchildren know the story as well. The story includes our childhood, places we have lived, some outstanding events in our lives, and some of our accomplishments, along with some trials we have faced throughout our lives. We have shared with you how we first met and how our lives were meant to be shared together forever. It's an incredible story, and we hope you will agree that it is a story that needed to be written.

*Our story was printed on beautifully decorated paper and placed in a nice binder, making it a keepsake for each of our children. They commented that it was a story they wanted to remember and were happy it had been recorded so it would always be told correctly.*

On the SEVENTH Day of

*Christmas*

We bring to you with love . . .

Embroidered Handkerchiefs! NeNa has made a beautiful embroidered hanky for each of our grandchildren. We hope this will be a treasured keepsake for you through the years and that you will have it with you on special occasions that occur in your life.

*An idea would be a white hanky on which you have embroidered a lovely border or the child's name or initials. This would be especially nice for a grandchild as well as your daughter or son. You could suggest to the grandchildren that this be kept to use on their baptism day, wedding day, or any special occasion in their lives. This could be handed down through the years. Who wouldn't love that?*

On the EIGHTH Day of

# Christmas

*We bring to you with love . . .*

Savings Bonds! Hopefully, this is a nice surprise for you. We were excited to give these to you at Christmas since most of us can use a little extra money at this time of the year. The value of the bonds has greatly increased through the years, and as you redeem the bonds, you will be amazed at their value. It is important that you invest your money wisely, but it is just as important that you invest your *time* wisely. Wisely invest both your time and your talents in your families. The day will come when you will receive your reward for such a wise investment . . . and how glorious shall be your reward.

*These were savings bonds we had purchased when each of our children were born. They had been put away with the thought that at some special time we would give them to our children. The message that accompanied them was instilled in my heart by a friend. She shared with me the rewards of wisely investing in her own family, and I knew right away that this was an invaluable concept to teach our children.*

You could also purchase savings bonds now and have the children and grandchildren watch as they mature and become more valuable. What a great way to teach the value of wise investments.

On the NINTH Day of

# Christmas

*We bring to you with love . . .*

Donuts! Here are some yummy, warm donuts to start off your day. We know how much you love them, so this is our special treat to you today. Enjoy!

*One Saturday morning, we showed up on the doorstep of each family with a box of warm donuts. This was a huge hit! You may want to purchase a gift certificate and have the family go together to get the donuts if you aren't able to be there. We attached a note to the previous day's gift telling them not to have breakfast the next day. There are many websites that offer to deliver all sorts of beautifully decorated cookies for various holidays.*

On the TENTH Day of

*Christmas*

*We bring to you with love . . .*

Reindeer Dust! Feed this treat to Santa's reindeer when he comes to visit. Take the reindeer dust and sprinkle it on your lawn before going to bed. The reindeer will be happy to have a treat just for them. Sweet dreams!

*We used dry oatmeal and mixed it with various colors of glitter to make this reindeer treat. Pint-size canning jars or empty baby food jars could be used. The instructions attached to each jar are included on the following page.*

## Secret Instructions for Reindeer Dust

Expecting a visit from Santa?
Here is a recipe I have found.
It is a special reindeer food
You sprinkle on the ground.
The oatmeal is for energy,
The sparkles are for flight,
So sprinkle the reindeer food
On Christmas Eve night!
All of Santa's reindeer
Love this healthy snack.
Next year Santa and his reindeer
Surely will be back!

—AUTHOR UNKNOWN

This is especially wonderful for young children. On Christmas Eve the grandchildren put on their pajamas, grab their jar of reindeer dust, and sprinkle it on the lawn before going to bed. They love the idea of feeding Santa's reindeer.

On the ELEVENTH Day of

Christmas

*We bring to you with love . . .*

A Kneeling Santa! Isn't this wonderful for us to be reminded that Santa also loves Jesus? Both Santa and Jesus are filled with love for us. We hope you will find a special place to put this on your memory tree. We should show our love for Jesus by being kind and good to one another. Always remember how much Jesus loves you. We love you too.

*In a local gift shop, we found a ceramic Santa kneeling in prayer at the manger of baby Jesus. These can also be purchased through the Internet. Be sure to allow for shipping time! The kneeling Santa gave us an opportunity to bring Santa into the true meaning of Christmas. A friend shared the verse on the following page with me, and I knew it would be perfect to enclose with the ceramic.*

## Santa's Plan

'Twas the night before Christmas and all through the house
Not a creature was stirring, not even a mouse.
And so goes the story about Christmas Eve
And the jolly old man in whom we believe.
Have you ever wondered how Santa came to be
So important to Christmas and to you and to me?
Well, it all began a long time ago
The night before Christ to earth was to go.

All prepared to make Christ's birth well announced
With angels and music and anthems pronounced.
But, alas, all had forgotten—in the final rush
How to make Christ's birthday remembered to us!
The kingdom was searched for the most excellent plan
That would help us remember God's gift to man.
A saintly old fellow, so jolly and gay
Came up with the best plan offered that day.

He said, "Send a fellow each year at this time
Who would help folks be happy and comfort their mind.
He could help them remember that God loves them so
By bringing presents to both friend and to foe.
He would show by example that true love and true joy
Comes only when shared with each girl and each boy."

Heaven decided Santa's plan was just right,
And Santa was asked to play the part that first night.
So from that first Christmas right down to today
When one heard the bells jingling and saw the big sleigh,
They knew it was Santa just making his way
To remind all the world of the love Jesus gave.
So, this night before Christmas, when you hear Santa come,
Remember he is doing this for the love of God's son.
And remember he teaches as did Christ of old
That to give of one's self is more precious than gold.

—ANONYMOUS

On the TWELFTH Day of

*Christmas*

*We bring to you with love . . .*

A Video of NeNa and PaPa Reading You Christmas Stories! We couldn't be in each of your homes, so you will have this video instead. We have chosen several stories to share with you. Get into your pajamas, wrap up in your Christmas quilt, and listen as we read to you. We love sharing time with you any way we can. Oh, how we love you.

*Some grandparents don't live close to their families, but there are ways you can still be together. This idea can bring you close during the holiday season and will become a treasured keepsake for your children. Choose several stories that you know they will love. Set up the video camera so both of you can be in the video. You could also record just your voice on a tape recorder. A few stories you may want to use are included on the following page.*

## The Little Gray Lamb

Once in a flock of sheep near Bethlehem there was a little lamb that was very unhappy. All the other lambs gambled about in the warm sunshine and played together, but this little lamb hardly left his mother's side and could not be persuaded to play with the others. Now the reason for this sadness was that while the other lambs had coats of snowy white, his fleece was a dingy, dirty gray. In vain the little lamb's mother told him that she loved him just as much as the white lambs. The others called to him to come and play.

"What do we care," they said, "whether your coat is white or gray? Come and play with us." But he only shook his head and shrank closer to his mother's side.

All around him in the fields were flowers nodding in the sunshine, with dazzling white petals. As he looked at them the little lamb begged, "Oh, beautiful flowers, will you not give me your white petals to cover me that my gray coat may be white?"

And the flowers laughed and replied, "Oh, little lamb, we cannot help you. If we should take our white petals from our stems, they would only wither and die. They will not make you white." So the little lamb sighed and walked away.

Again he looked up into the bright blue sky and saw the white clouds floating there and cried, "Oh fleecy white clouds, won't you please come down and wrap yourselves around me, so that my gray coat will be white?"

Then the clouds gently said, "No, little lamb, if we should come down to earth we would turn into mist and rain. We would cover your gray coat, but it would not make it white."

Again as he lay by his mother's side at night and saw the stars twinkling in the sky, the little lamb pleaded, "Oh beautiful stars, won't you come and fasten yourselves to my gray coat, that it may be white and shinning as you are?"

But the stars, looking calmly down, replied, "Oh little lamb, we guide travelers over the great desert and sailors over the wide sea. We do our work in the world, and it matters not to us what our color is. Be content with your gray coat, for nothing will ever make it white."

One night as the little gray lamb lay as usual beside his mother, watching the bright stars, he noticed a wonderful light in the sky, far in the distance; then, even as he watched, it grew nearer and brighter. At first no one else saw it, but then all the sheep noticed it and wondered what it could be. Brighter and still brighter it grew, until it became almost blinding. The shepherds and sheep heard strange and beautiful music like nothing they had ever heard before. The shining angels appeared, singing as they came. The shepherds were frightened and threw themselves on their faces to shut out the radiance, while the sheep huddled together, hiding their heads in each others' wool—all but the little gray lamb.

Then from the band of shining angels came the most beautiful voice ever heard on earth, "Fear not: for behold, I bring you good tidings of great joy, which shall be to all people. For unto you is born this day in the City of David a Savior, which is Christ the Lord. And this shall be a sign unto you; Ye shall find the babe wrapped in swaddling clothes, lying in a manger."

Then the light began to fade, and the angels slowly withdrew from sight. The shepherds raised their heads, and said, "Let us go, even unto Bethlehem as the angels said." So leaving their flocks still huddled together, they started for the little town just over the hills, and behind them, unnoticed all the way, followed the little gray lamb. At last the shepherds came to a cave just outside the inn, and entering with them the little lamb saw a tiny baby lying in his mother's arms—a baby with a beautiful light on his face! The shepherds knelt before the baby. The little lamb, his heart beating fast with a strange fear, crept closer and closer until at last he stood beside the baby . Then the tiny fingers unclasped their hold of the mother and reached out. The little lamb hardly dared to breathe, but he stood very still. In a moment, the baby's eyes softly closed, and he was asleep.

The shepherds arose and went their way, but the little lamb dared not follow them for he was afraid that if he moved, he would awaken the baby. The mother fell asleep and the father also, and only the little lamb was awake. He did not dare to sleep for fear some movement he made would awaken the baby; so, cramped and stiff, trying hard not to go to sleep, he stood motionless. The night grew darker and darker, and then toward morning it began to lighten again, and the little lamb thought of his mother and the quiet pasture on the hillside. How tired he was, and how he did wish he could stretch his cramped little legs and lie down beside her. At last the baby stirred and unclasped his fingers; the little lamb slowly made his way to the entrance of the cave. Then as the first rays of morning light fell upon him, he saw that a wonderful thing had happened. The touch of the baby Jesus had made his gray wool a beautiful, wonderful white.

—AUTHOR UNKNOWN

## Christmas Roses

Bobby was getting cold sitting out in his backyard in the snow. Bobby didn't wear boots; he didn't like them and anyway, he didn't own any. The thin sneakers he wore had a few holes in them and they did a poor job of keeping out the cold. Bobby had been in the backyard for about an hour already. And, try as he might, he could not come up with an idea for his mother's Christmas gift. He shook his head as he thought, *This is useless. Even if I do come up with an idea, I don't have any money to spend.*

Ever since his father had passed away three years ago, the family of five had struggled. It wasn't because his mother didn't care or didn't try; there just never seemed to be enough. She worked nights at the hospital, but the small wage that she was earning could only be stretched so far. What the family lacked in money and material things, they more than made up for in love and family unity.

Bobby had two older sisters and one younger sister who ran the household in their mother's absence. All three of his sisters had already made beautiful gifts for their mother. Somehow, it just wasn't fair. Here it was Christmas Eve already and he had nothing. Wiping a tear from his eye, Bobby kicked the snow and started to walk down to the street where the shops and stores were. It wasn't easy being six without a father, especially when he needed a man to talk to.

Bobby walked from shop to shop looking into each decorated window. Everything seemed so beautiful and out of reach. It was starting to get dark, so Bobby reluctantly turned to walk home when, suddenly, his eyes caught the glimmer of the setting sun's rays reflecting off of something along the curb. He reached down and discovered a shiny dime. Never before has anyone felt so wealthy as Bobby felt at that moment.

As he held his new-found treasure, a warmth spread through his entire body, and he walked into the first store he saw. His excitement quickly turned cold when the salesperson told him that he couldn't buy anything with only a dime. He saw a flower shop and went inside to wait in line. When the shop owner asked if he could help him, Bobby presented the dime and asked if he could buy one flower for his mother's Christmas gift. The shop owner looked at Bobby and his ten-cent offering. Then he put his hand on Bobby's shoulder and said to him, "You just wait here and I'll see what I can do for you." As Bobby waited, he looked at the beautiful flowers, and even though he was a boy, he could see why mothers and girls liked flowers. The sound of the door closing as the last customer left jolted Bobby back to reality. All alone in the shop, Bobby began to feel alone and afraid. Suddenly, the shop owner came out and moved to the counter. There, before Bobby's eyes, lay twelve long-stem, red roses, with delicate green leaves and tiny white flowers all tied together with a big silver bow. Bobby's heart sank as the owner picked them up and placed them gently into a long white box.

"That will be ten cents, young man," the shop owner said, reaching out his hand for the dime. Slowly, Bobby moved his hand to give the man his dime. Could this be true? No one else would give him a thing for his dime! Sensing the boy's reluctance, the shop owner added, "I just happened to have some roses on sale for ten cents a dozen. Would you like them?" This time Bobby did not hesitate, and when the man placed the long box into his hands, he knew it was true. Walking out the door that the owner was holding for Bobby, he heard the shopkeeper say, "Merry Christmas, son."

As the shopkeeper returned inside, his wife walked out into the shop. "Who were you talking to back there, and where are the roses you were preparing?"

Staring out the window and blinking the tears from his own eyes, he replied, "A strange thing happened to me this morning. While I was setting up things to open the shop, I thought I heard a voice telling me to set aside a dozen of my best roses for a special gift. I wasn't sure at the time whether I had lost my mind or what, but I set them aside anyway. Then just a few minutes ago a little boy came into the shop and wanted to buy a flower for his mother with one small dime. When I looked at him, I saw myself, many years ago. I too was a poor boy with nothing to buy my mother a Christmas gift. A bearded man whom I never knew stopped me on the street and told me that he wanted to give me ten dollars. When I saw that little boy tonight, I knew who that voice was, and I put together a dozen of my very best roses." The shop owner and his wife hugged each other tightly, and as they stepped out into the bitter cold air, they somehow didn't feel cold at all.

—AUTHOR UNKNOWN

## Levi's Christmas

Young Levi Sawyer was tall for his age; perhaps this is why the townspeople didn't see the lonely child within the large frame. He lived with his father—at least, that is where he was supposed to live. His father was a drinker. Perhaps he was not a bad man, just one with a weakness, but most often he left Levi to fend for himself. Sometimes Levi was hungry. One day he found a can of salmon that had been thrown away. He ate the entire thing in one sitting. Later he threw up the contents of his hurried lunch.

He dreaded Christmas. It wasn't because he didn't believe in Christmas or Santa Claus; it was because they didn't seem to believe in him. As the season approached he would pull his tattered coat around his shoulders and walk through the crunching snow. He would walk past the homes in the small southern Utah community and look longingly into the unshuttered front windows at the happy people inside. They were gathered around their Christmas trees or singing carols around the spinet pianos inside their parlors, and good smells of Christmas were in the air. The young lad could only linger outside and imagine what it would be like to be included in a real home, with a real family.

Each year the town would gather at the local meetinghouse for a community Christmas party. There would be a tree, and the parents would bring one gift for each of their children and place it on this tree. Levi had gone to these parties before. He enjoyed them. He liked the singing, the friendly greetings he received . . . the people were never unkind to him, just unaware. It was warm inside the church, and each child was given a treat: a popcorn ball or perhaps a paper bag full of peanuts (with shells) and a little hard tack candy. The peanut shells would stick to the candy, but that didn't matter. They tasted like Christmas to the children.

But Levi dreaded it when it was time for the presents to be distributed. There was never a gift for him. He would try to leave unnoticed before the other children could see that he had been forgotten again. This year Levi had plans to leave before the distribution was even started. But there was something inside him, a tiny hope that perhaps there would be a small token for him. Rhoana Hatch, a pretty girl who he admired was there. Her father, Meltair, never forgot to have a present for his children. Levi watched as Rhoana accepted her gift from the tree.

She glanced shyly at Levi and gave him a smile. This tall, lanky lad held a special place in her young girl heart. She too wished that this year would be different for him. The tree was starting to look quite bare when Levi noticed something shiny toward the back, a pair of ice skates. Wow, whoever got those would be lucky! Levi would slide on the frozen pond with his shoes, but that was not the same. Wouldn't that be wonderful to own a pair of real skates and race with the other boys?

A name was called out . . . no, he must have heard wrong. Did they say "Levi"? He listened once more . . . yes, he had heard right.

"Levi? Levi Sawyer, these skates are for you," the man acting as Santa called out.

Eagerly, but a little fearful, he went forward to receive the prize. He tried not to act too excited; it could be a mistake. But there was no mistake. This year Levi had not been forgotten. The skates on the tree were for him. He looked them over with awe and then put them under his coat as he went out into the cold night air. There was a new spring in his step and a smile on his face. Someone remembered him, someone cared.

Young Rhoana smiled too, as she watched Levi's Uncle Tom leave the party. He, too, had a spring in his step and a smile on his face, for he had seen the loneliness of his brother's son and had found a way to let him know he was loved and had not been forgotten.

—JOYCE KAY GOODRICH

# Chapter Five

## *Our Favorite Things*

*"Grandmothers hold their grandchildren's tiny hands for just a moment but hold their hearts forever."*

—AUTHOR UNKNOWN

Each year brings the challenge of surprising the family with some new ideas for the 12 Days of Christmas. One afternoon while watching Oprah's TV show and her Christmas giveaway of her favorite things, I began to imagine the excitement of sharing with our family *our* favorite things. We told our family that we wouldn't be comparing our gifts to those of Oprah, but we would love sharing those things that were special to us. So here are some of "Our Favorite Things" we shared during the 12 Days of Christmas.

On the FIRST Day of

# Christmas

*We bring to you with love . . .*

A Sack of Idaho Potatoes! Yes, today you are receiving a huge sack of Idaho potatoes, straight from Uncle Blaine's farm. We promise these will be the best potatoes you have had for a long time. Idaho potatoes are undoubtedly one of our favorite things.

*Sterling was born and raised in Idaho and has a great love for true Idaho french fries! Our children and grandchildren love PaPa's homemade fries, so we gave each family a sack of Idaho spuds (as a true Idahoan refers to potatoes), along with a bottle of Sterling's favorite peanut oil. We even included a bottle of fry sauce and a bottle of ketchup. Think of foods that are relevant to your area of the country or that are your favorites and include them in your 12 Days of Christmas.*

On the SECOND Day of

# Christmas

*We bring to you with love . . .*

Pancake Mix and Syrup! We know how you love for us to prepare homemade pancakes for breakfast when you stay overnight with us. Pancakes are definitely one of our favorite things, so we're sharing some mix and syrup with you today. Enjoy making and eating these together.

*Our family loves pancakes at family reunions, so we wrapped a big bag of pancake mix and a bottle of our favorite syrup for one of the 12 Days of Christmas. They were reminded of the fun we have when we get together. We hold tight to those memories.*

On the THIRD Day of

# Christmas

*We bring to you with love . . .*

## A Gift Certificate to Our Favorite Restaurant!

Tonight we will be treating you to dinner at one of our favorite restaurants. This will be an evening of neither cooking nor cleaning for Mom! You *know* this is one of our favorite things to do.

*There are many variations to this idea. Consider showing up at their door with your favorite homemade casserole or having a pizza delivered to their home. One year we met at a Saturday breakfast buffet and let the grandchildren choose whatever they wanted for breakfast. They loved being with their cousins and eating as much as their little tummies could hold. This was definitely a favorite choice since Sterling and I got to spend time with both our children and grandchildren.*

On the FOURTH Day of

*Christmas*

*We bring to you with love . . .*

**Unexpected Money!** Here are a few extra dollars to help with those added expenses during the holidays. We can remember through the years how just having a little extra money during Christmas would have lightened our load a lot. One of our favorite things is helping our children and making your load a little lighter also.

*Some of our children were attending college and trying to support their families at the same time, so we decided to give them a little extra money for the holidays. That would definitely have been one of our favorite things to receive when our children were young! We remember how a little unexpected money could be like a dream come true. It doesn't need to be a large sum of money, but enough perhaps for movie tickets for Mom and Dad and to pay a babysitter.*

On the FIFTH Day of

*Christmas*

*We bring to you with love . . .*

## A Contribution to the Heifer Foundation!

Today we want to give you another of our favorite things. We have donated money and purchased a sheep in our family's name. This sheep will be given to a family in another country who will take care of the sheep and sell the wool from the sheep to purchase food and clothing for their family. You will be helping this family every day throughout the year. The true spirit of Christmas is service to others. We are also enclosing a tiny toy sheep for you to place somewhere in your home so it can serve to remind you each day of the service you are giving. We appreciate the opportunities we have to serve others and consider it one of our favorite things.

*You can gather more information on The Heifer Foundation by writing Heifer Project International, 1015 Louisiana Street, Little Rock, Arkansas 72202 or on www.heifer.org.*

On the SIXTH Day of

# Christmas

*We bring to you with love . . .*

Homemade Fudge! Surprise! You are receiving your second batch of NeNa's fudge. We know it is one of your favorite things, and it definitely is one of ours. Thanks for making *our* favorite things *your* favorites also. Enjoy, and remember how much you are loved.

*As I stated earlier, homemade fudge is always part of the gift for Day 1. Well, one of the grandchildren made the comment that they wished NeNa and PaPa thought two tins of fudge was one of their favorite things. Oh, the joy these children bring.*

# Fudge

2 cups sugar

13 large marshmallows

⅔ cup evaporated milk

6 oz. chocolate chips

½ cup butter (not margarine)

1 tsp. pure vanilla

nuts to taste

In large skillet, mix together sugar, marshmallows, and evaporated milk. Dissolve and bring to a boil. Stirring constantly, time for *exactly* 3 minutes after boiling begins. Remove from heat and add the remainder of the ingredients. Stir until the butter and chocolate chips have melted well. Pour into a lightly buttered dish and refrigerate until cool. Cut into squares.

*I bet you were waiting for some secret ingredient that makes my fudge special. No, but for some reason our children and grandchildren consider my fudge their favorite. I'll keep making it each year knowing it means so much to them . . . and I'll keep adding lots of love.*

On the SEVENTH Day of
# Christmas
*We bring to you with love . . .*

A Disposable Camera! Sometimes in the rush of things we forget to take Christmas pictures, so today we want you to take a whole roll of pictures of your decorations, one another, the children, and whatever else you feel is important. We have also included a snow globe in which you can put your favorite picture of the Christmas season. Hopefully this will be a special memory for you. *You* give us cherished memories.

*One of our favorite things is having pictures of our family so we can continue holding tight to our memories.*

On the EIGHTH Day of

# Christmas

*We bring to you with love . . .*

Scrapbooking Supplies! We have put together all the things you will need to make a Christmas page for your scrapbook. What a great way to remember this special Christmas. Have fun designing it together.

*Scrapbooking is a very popular gift idea for one of the 12 Days of Christmas. Put together a package for a Christmas scrapbook page for their album. Perhaps it could be centered on a special time you spent together. One of our favorite things is having beautiful pictures of our family.*

On the NINTH Day of

# Christmas

*We bring to you with love . . .*

The Christmas Jar! Please read this book, *The Christmas Jar*, together as a family and share the sweet spirit in the book. We hope you will be excited to have a Christmas Jar in your own homes. The idea of contributing to the jar all during the year helps us remember the importance of service to others.

*Give each family a decorated, quart-size canning jar with "The Christmas Jar" painted on it. Tell them to put it where it can be seen throughout the year. They are to use the jar daily to collect extra money they may have, and as the holidays approach, they will join together as a family and choose someone who could use the money in their Christmas Jar.*

We also gave them a copy of the book *The Christmas Jar* by Jason F. Wright and asked that they read this tender story. Hopefully having the Christmas Jar where it can easily be seen will continue to remind them of the need to help others during the Christmas season and throughout the year.

\* \* \*

*I wish we could put up some of the Christmas spirit in jars and open a jar of it every month.*

—HARLAN MILLER

On the TENTH Day of

# Christmas

*We bring to you with love . . .*

A Book Especially for Your Family! We gave a lot of thought to the book we would choose for your family. Hopefully it is one that will have special meaning for you. Reading good books is important, and especially those that have special meaning to us.

*I remember how much we enjoyed choosing a special book that would fit each individual family. We considered their needs and tried to find a book that would fit the ages of the children.*

Heather, one of our daughters, shared this with us:

"I gathered our boys around me on a particularly cold and snowy December morning and told them I wanted to read them the book they had been given that day. I began to read about a young boy who was scared about growing up and leaving home. He didn't want to leave his mommy, although he knew the day would come when he would have to leave her. This had the attention of each of my sons, from age three to age eleven. As I continued to read, the tears welled up in my eyes and quickly made their way down my cheeks. I tried to wipe them away without bringing attention to myself when I noticed that my little boys were also touched by the spirit of that wonderful story. When I finished reading the book, two of the boys ran to their bedroom and came back with a gift they had made for me in school. Each boy kissed me and shyly gave me their small gift."

Yes, they wanted to show love for their mommy that day. Indeed, the purpose of the 12 Days of Christmas was being fulfilled . . . and this was another of our favorite things.

On the ELEVENTH Day of

# Christmas

*We bring to you with love . . .*

**An Evening of Babysitting!** Tonight Mom and Dad can have an evening to themselves. NeNa and PaPa will be there to tend the children! Have a great evening, and know that we are enjoying the extra time with our grandchildren.

*The parents will love the extra time to finish their shopping without children around, and you will have an evening with your grandchildren to make wonderful Christmas memories. This is a great gift of your time . . . and definitely one of our favorite things.*

On the TWELFTH Day of

# Christmas

*We bring to you with love . . .*

A Family Picture Puzzle . . . We know how much you love putting puzzles together, so we had a very special puzzle made for you. This puzzle is extra special because it has on it the face of each member of your family. Each one of you is special to us.

*Have a puzzle made from a picture of the family. Your grandchildren will think it is wonderful—putting together a puzzle with their little faces on it! Check around. There are definitely photo shops that can do this for you. You will need to have the picture enlarged and then laminated. Check with your local photo developing store or search on the Internet for instructions.*

# Chapter Six

*"Behold Your Little Ones"*

*"Two little children were put early to bed on a winter's night, for the fire had gone out, and the cold was pouring in at the many cracks of their frail shanty. The mother strove to keep out the scantiness of the bed covering by placing clean boards over the children. A pair of bright eyes shone out from under a board, and just before it was hushed in slumber, a sweet voice said, "Mother, how nice this is. How I pity the poor people who don't have any boards to cover their children with on this cold night."*

—Author Unknown

This theme was definitely one that Sterling and I spent many hours planning. During the year several of our children and their spouses had come to us with concerns about teaching their little children and making sure they are fortified with all they need to know to face problems in the world today. We assured them they are doing a marvelous job and praised them for making their children the most important part of their lives. We reminded them of the great love our Heavenly Father has for them and for their children. Sterling and I decided to dedicate that year's 12 Days of Christmas to the grandchildren. Yes, it was their year. Everything was centered around the grandchildren and how special they are to us all. Thus the theme: "Behold Your Little Ones."

On the FIRST Day of

*Christmas*

We bring to you with love . . .

"Behold Your Little Ones" Plaque! We have made a plaque for you to display in your home. Please put it where it can be seen daily to serve as a reminder of just how important these little ones really are. Wouldn't the plaque look great with pictures of your "little ones" around it? They are more precious than words can describe.

*We wanted this year's theme displayed in each home, so we found someone who makes beautiful wooden signs and we ordered a sign that read "Behold Your Little Ones" for each family. We chose a lovely font that would compliment the wording.*

On the SECOND Day of

# Christmas

*We bring to you with love . . .*

A New CD! We are excited with your gift for today because it is music, and we have always felt that powerful messages can be taught through music. You'll want to listen closely to the words of this song and, again, be reminded of just how precious our little ones really are. Enjoy the time you have with them and the opportunities you have to teach them—and, yes, "let them be little."

*It has always seemed to me that you can say more through music than any other way. I envy those who can write and sing these incredible songs. There is a wonderful song entitled "Let Them Be Little" by Billie Dean. I had heard the song several times during the year, and each time I thought that it was absolutely perfect for the 12 Days of Christmas. At that point I wasn't sure just how it was going to be used, but I knew I had to use it somehow.*

When the idea of the theme "Behold Your Little Ones" came to me, it all started fitting together. The words of the song are beautiful and touched the hearts of the parents just as they had touched Sterling and me. The song talks about giving children love and praise every day and letting them enjoy being little. What perfect advice from a wonderful song. Perhaps it takes becoming a grandparent to appreciate how quickly the years fly by when children are small. We shared with our children how important it is to enjoy every day with these precious little ones and to "Let Them Be Little."

On the THIRD Day of

# Christmas

*We bring to you with love . . .*

A Christmas Get-away! We are giving you this gift a little early so you can get excited making plans with us. We will be taking your family with us to a lovely cabin at Bear Lake, where we will all be together for a few days. We will have lots of fun playing games, watching special Christmas movies together, eating our favorite foods, snowmobiling, playing in the snow, and just having a marvelous time together. We can hardly wait to see your beautiful faces coming through the door. Doesn't it sound just perfect? Merry Christmas to our family.

*Since this was the year dedicated to the little ones, we decided to plan something just for them. We rented a cabin in a nearby resort, and our entire family went there on Christmas night and stayed for several days. Oh, what a thrill seeing our little ones having such a grand time together.*

This could also be done by opening your own home for a Christmas get-together. Our family is too large for any of our homes to hold us all. Plan lots of special events for the children and prepare many of their favorite foods.

This was the main gift for each family, and they loved it. The other days had smaller items that weren't very costly. Naturally we had to tell the parents about our get-away earlier in the year so they could make arrangements to be off work for several days. This was the crowning event for the grandchildren, and they especially loved that it was planned just for them.

On the FOURTH Day of

# Christmas

*We bring to you with love . . .*

Christmas in a Can! Tonight you can share all the things inside your Christmas can. You'll find some yummy treats. We will be thinking of you.

*Some ideas for your Christmas Can are included on the following pages.*

# Christmas Can

Take a clean, unused gallon paint can with a handle and cover the outside with Christmas craft paper. Add any extra decorations that would make the can festive. On the top of the lid, glue a decorated paper that lists the ingredients inside. Place inside the can the following:

 ❋1 pkg. wassail mix *(recipe below)*
 ❋1 box spice cookie mix *(instructions below)*
 ❋1 Christmas ornament *(one that goes along with the theme)*
 ❋1 pkg. microwave popcorn *(try kettle corn!)*
 ❋1 box hot cocoa mix *(or make your own mix)*
 ❋1 Christmas story *(your choice or one included here)*

## Wassail

2 cups Tang

1 (3 oz.) pkg. pre-sweetened lemonade mix

1⅓ cups sugar

1 tsp. cinnamon

½ tsp. ground cloves

Combine all ingredients and mix well. The wassail mix can be put into small cellophane bags and stapled shut.

❋*Add a small card with the instructions for use: Keeps up to 6 months. Use 2 to 3 teaspoons of mix with 1 cup hot water.*

## Spice Cookie Mix

1 box spice cake mix

1 egg

2 Tbsp. water

2 Tbsp. flour

¼ cup soft shortening

Place a label on a box of spice cake mix with these instructions:

Add all ingredients together. It will make a stiff dough. Mix well and chill dough. Roll out on floured surface and cut with cookie cutters into your favorite shapes. Place on baking sheet and bake at 375 degrees for 8 to 10 minutes. Decorate as desired.

*This idea could also be used for other occasions. If you have someone away from home—a college student, missionary, or someone in the military—you could send them lots of treats in a decorated paint can. What a great way to show you care and are thinking of them.*

## The Trucker

During the Roosevelt era, times were tough. The president was promising a brighter moon, but the Beasleys hadn't seen it rise over their small town in the Texas panhandle. So when he got the call that his son was ill in California and not expected to live, Bill Beasley didn't know how he was going to scrape together the money for his wife and himself to make the trip.

Bill had worked as a trucker his entire life, but he never managed to accumulate any savings. Swallowing his pride, he phoned a few close relatives for help, but they were no better off.

So it was with embarrassment and dejection that Bill Beasley walked the mile from his house to the filling station and told the owner, "My son is really sick," he said, "and I've got no cash. Can you trust me for the phone call to California?"

"Pick up the phone and talk as long as you need to," was the reply.

As he started to dial, he was interrupted by a voice behind him asking, "Aren't you Bill Beasley?"

It was a stranger, jumping down from the cab of a truck with out-of-state plates. The young man didn't look familiar, and Bill could only stare at him with a puzzled look and say, "That's right, I am."

"Your son was one of my best pals when we were growing up together. When I went off to college, I lost all track of him." He paused for a moment and then continued, "Heard you say he's sick?"

"Real bad from what we hear. I'm gonna call and try to make some arrangements for the wife to get out there with him." Then, as a matter of courtesy, he added, "Have yourself a Merry Christmas. Wish your daddy was still with us."

Old man Beasley walked into the office of the station and placed his call to the cousin on the West coast, informing him that he or his wife hoped to be out as soon as possible. There was an obvious look of sorrow on the elder citizen's face as he assured the owner that he would pay for the call as soon as he could.

"The call has been paid for. That trucker—the one your son used to pal around with—left me a twenty and said to give you the change when the phone bill comes in. He also left you this envelope."

The old man fumbled open the envelope and pulled out two sheets of paper. One read, "You were the first trucker I ever traveled with, the first my dad trusted enough to let me go along with when I was barely five years old. I remember you bought me a Snickers bar."

The second sheet, much smaller in size, was a signed check with an attached message: "Fill out the amount needed for you and your wife to make the trip—and give your son, my pal, a Snickers bar. Merry Christmas!"

—Author Unknown

## No Santa Claus?

I remember my first Christmas adventure with Grandma. I was just a kid. I remember tearing across town on my bike to visit her on the day my big sister dropped the bomb: "There is no Santa Claus," she jeered. "Even dummies know that!"

My Grandma was not the gushy kind, never had been. I fled to her that day because I knew she would be straight with me. I knew Grandma always told the truth, and I knew that the truth always went down a whole lot easier when swallowed with one of her "world famous" cinnamon buns. I knew they were world famous because Grandma said so. It had to be true. Grandma was home and the buns were still warm. Between bites, I told her everything. She was ready for me. "No Santa Claus?" she snorted. "Ridiculous! Don't believe it. That rumor has been going around for years, and it makes me mad, plain mad! Now put on your coat and let's go."

"Go? Go where, Grandma?" I asked. I hadn't even finished my second world famous cinnamon bun!

"Where" turned out to be Kerby's General Store, the one store in town that had a little bit of just about everything. As we walked through its doors, Grandma handed me ten dollars. That was a bundle in those days.

"Take this money," she said, "and buy something for someone who needs it. I'll wait for you in the car."

Then she turned and walked out of Kerby's. I was only eight years old. I'd often gone shopping with my mother, but never had I shopped for anything all by myself. The store seemed big and crowded, full of people scrambling to finish their Christmas shopping. For a few moments I just stood there, confused, clutching that ten dollar bill, wondering what to buy and who on earth to buy it for!

I thought of everybody I knew: my family, my friends, my neighbors, the kids at school, the people who went to my church. I was just about thought out, when I suddenly thought of Bobby Decker. He was a kid with bad breath and messy hair, and he sat right behind me in Mrs. Pollock's grade two class. Bobby Decker didn't have a coat. I knew that because he never went out to recess during the winter. His mother always wrote a note telling the teacher that he had a cough but all we kids knew that Bobby Decker didn't have a cough; he had no good coat.

I fingered the ten dollar bill with growing excitement. I would buy Bobby Decker a coat!

I settled on a red corduroy one that had a hood to it. It looked real warm, and he would like that. "Is this a Christmas present for someone?" the lady behind the counter asked kindly as I laid my ten dollars down.

"Yes, ma'am," I replied shyly. "It's for Bobby."

The nice lady smiled at me as I told her about how Bobby really needed a good winter coat. I didn't get any change, but she put the coat in a bag, smiled again, and wished me a Merry Christmas.

That evening Grandma helped me wrap the coat in Christmas paper and ribbons. A little tag fell out of the coat and Grandma tucked it in her Bible. On a Christmas tag we wrote, "To Bobby, From Santa Claus." Grandma said that Santa always insisted on secrecy. Then she drove me over to Bobby Decker's house, explaining as we went that I was now and forever officially one of Santa's helpers. Grandma parked down the street from Bobby's house, and she and I crept noiselessly and hid in the bushes by his front walk. Then Grandma gave me a nudge. "All right, Santa Claus," she whispered, "get going."

I took a deep breath, dashed for his front door, threw the present down on his step, pounded his doorbell, and flew back to the safety of the bushes and Grandma. Together we waited breathlessly in the darkness for the front door to open. Finally it did, and there stood Bobby.

Fifty years haven't dimmed the thrill of those moments spent shivering beside my grandma in Bobby Decker's bushes. That night, I realized that those awful rumors about Santa Claus were just what Grandma said they were: ridiculous! Santa was alive and well, and we were on his team. I still have the Bible, with the coat tag tucked inside . . . $19.95.

—AUTHOR UNKNOWN

On the FIFTH Day of

# Christmas

*We bring to you with love . . .*

A Journal! Today each member of your family is receiving a new journal to begin using in the New Year. We want to encourage you to continue keeping a daily record of the happenings in your life. It is important to record the daily events plus your feelings about all that is going on in your life. It will be invaluable to you in the years to come.

*This is a great way to encourage our children and grandchildren to keep a journal. They will thank you in the years to come. There are many lovely journals available at local bookstores and gift shops. You can make the journals extra special by having them engraved.*

On the SIXTH Day of

# Christmas

*We bring to you with love . . .*

Holiday Music! Today you are receiving a new Christmas CD. We know you love to have Christmas music playing in your homes, so we have chosen a new CD for you. This is one that is especially for the children, so enjoy it together. Sing along and have a happy day.

*Our family loves holiday music, and we are guilty of playing it quite early in the year. Sterling and I start shopping for a new holiday CD for the families as soon as they hit the stores. We try to find ones that the whole family will enjoy—and one that will leave a sweet message of Christmas in the home.*

On the SEVENTH Day of

*Christmas*

*We bring to you with love . . .*

Matching Pajama Pants! You are going to look adorable in these new pajama pants. They will keep you warm
on these cold, snowy nights and will also make a darling
picture. We will look forward to seeing a picture of your
family in your matching Christmassy pajama pants.

*This was one of their favorites. Be sure to give this gift early so they can*
*be worn and appreciated all during the season. You could also sew the*
*pajamas, which would assure that you get all the sizes you need. Any*
*fabric store will have pajama patterns, so you can choose the style that*
*best suits your family. You can include matching T-shirts if you want:*
*boys matching in one color and the girls in another.*

On the EIGHTH Day of

# Christmas

*We bring to you with love . . .*

Baking Cookies with NeNa! Since you children don't have school today, NeNa will be picking you up for a day of baking cookies together. Be sure to bring your Christmas aprons. We'll have such a wonderful time!

*What a perfect morning for grandma and the grandchildren! This takes a little organization on grandma's part, but it is certainly worth it. If there are lots of grandchildren involved, you may want to make this a two-morning project. Keep in mind the ages of the children and how much help they are going to need.*

After you have finished baking and decorating the cookies, place them on Christmas paper plates, cover them with cellophane paper, tie a pretty bow around the cellophane, and have the children deliver the cookies to people who are special in their lives: friends, teachers, or neighbors.

## Peanut Butter Cookies

⅔ cup firmly packed brown sugar

½ cup margarine, softened

½ cup peanut butter (chunky or smooth)

1 egg

½ cup regular Cream of Wheat

1 tsp. vanilla extract

1 ¼ cups all-purpose flour

½ tsp. baking soda

In medium bowl with electric mixer, beat brown sugar, peanut butter, margarine, and egg until fluffy; blend in cereal and vanilla. Stir in flour and baking soda to make a stiff dough. Shape dough into 1-inch balls. Place 2 inches apart on greased baking sheets. Flatten balls with bottom of floured glass; press with fork tines to make crises-cross pattern. Bake at 350 degrees for 8 to 9 minutes or until lightly browned. Remove from sheets and let cool on wire racks. Makes 4 dozen cookies.

✳*We sometimes add chocolate chips to this batter and it is delicious!*

On the NINTH Day of

# Christmas

*We bring to you with love . . .*

A Visit to a Local Nursing Home! Tonight our family will join together and visit a nursing home in our area. The people there are wonderful, but they are lonely and need visitors at this time of the year. They will love seeing you and hearing your sweet voices as we sing carols to them. We can hardly wait to share this evening with you.

*Our children and grandchildren enjoyed this evening as much as any other we have experienced. We all met at a local nursing home and sang carols and shared conversation with the residents. We were amazed at the joy these sweet people felt with us just being there and sharing our time with them. One year we took cookies we had made together. They were more appreciative than we could have imagined, and we came away with the true spirit of Christmas in our hearts.*

On the TENTH Day of

*Christmas*

*We bring to you with love . . .*

Personalized Books for the Children! We have a great surprise for you today. You are receiving your own personalized book, one with your very own name in it. We think this will become one of your favorite books during the holiday season. We love you so much.

*The Internet has many sites that sell personalized books. We chose the book* Baby Jesus *and had it personalized with the name of each child in the family. Our grandchildren have loved having the books read to them and hearing their own names used in the story. We also included names of their cousins, so that made it even more fun.*

On the ELEVENTH Day of
Christmas
*We bring to you with love . . .*

A Candy Bar Cake! Isn't this a great treat! We have tried to include all of your favorite candy bars, so look for the one you like the most. You may want to invite a friend over to share your candy bar cake. Have fun!

*To make the candy bar cakes, you use one 12-inch piece and one 6-inch piece of Styrofoam, each about 2 inches thick. Glue the 6-inch piece on top of the 12-inch piece; then glue miniature candy bars all along the sides of your "cake." Cover the tops of both pieces with curly ribbons. It's such a fun idea and the children loved it. Of course, they like anything involving candy. We used their favorite candy bars and made it colorful.*

On the TWELFTH Day of
# Christmas
*We bring to you with love . . .*

A Visit With Santa . . . What a special day! Our plans today will be to pick up the grandchildren at noon and head to the mall. We will have lunch and then visit Santa and have their pictures taken. This is such a special day for us to be able to see our grandchildren interact with Santa. We enjoy having pictures each year to compare how you grandchildren have grown.

*Most malls have a Santa site, so this is a really fun experience to share with the grandchildren. Perhaps grandma and grandpa could also be in the picture. Now wouldn't that be a keepsake to treasure!*

# Chapter Seven

## Our Family Indian Tribe

*"Do your best now . . . don't save it for a special occasion"*

—JAMES E. TALMAGE

About five years ago, while living in another state, we met Lincoln and Janet and immediately became great friends. We visited their cabin and noticed a large tepee in the side yard. We were full of questions about how the tepee was used. They told us they had organized an Indian tribe for their family, and they hold tribal meetings in the tepee. I was hanging on every word. This was something that would fit our family perfectly.

Sterling and I began planning our own Indian tribe. We took the first part of each of our last names, and this became the name of our tribe— Vangiawa Pingca (Van Orden, Giacalone, Watson, Pingree, and Call)! There was lots of excitement in our family when we announced this. Sterling has the title of Indian chief and I am his squaw.

We planned a family reunion during the summer and dedicated one of the evenings to organizing our tribe. Each family was assigned a color. The colors we chose were green, blue, yellow, red, orange, and purple. We had balloons in each color plus headbands with feathers of the same colors. Our friends loaned us a beautiful Indian headdress for our chief to wear that evening.

Our two sons sat in the middle of the room beating on drums as the families entered the room. This set the mood. Each person was instructed to choose an Indian name. How fun to watch and listen as they decided on their name and as they made sure it pertained to something that would identify them. At the end of the evening we turned out the lights and, while waving glow-in-the-dark sticks, we sang songs about our family being an eternal family and about each one of us being a child of God.

Now they ask us constantly, "When are we going to have another family tribal meeting?"

Sterling and I have used these get-togethers to impress upon our children and grandchildren how important our family is to us and that we need to always remember that our choices can affect our entire family, whether it is for good or bad. Our "chief" has the opportunity to teach valuable principles to our family. We hope our family Indian tribe will continue to bond us closer together in a fun way. Our Vangiawa Pingca family Indian tribe led to another idea for our 12 Days of Christmas.

On the FIRST Day of

# Christmas

*We bring to you with love . . .*

Matching Sweatshirts! What fun we had planning our family Indian tribe. Each individual family was assigned a color just for them. Today you are each receiving a sweatshirt in the color assigned to your family. It's going to be such fun wearing these when we hold our next tribal meeting. You'll look great.

*Matching sweatshirts could be used for any occasion. You may want to print a family picture or use iron-on patches and letters on the sweatshirts. Our Indian tribe name was printed on T-shirts one year, and family pictures were taken. Give a T-shirt or sweatshirt as one of the 12 Days of Christmas and also use it for a family reunion.*

On the SECOND Day of
**Christmas**
*We bring to you with love . . .*

Trail Mix! This bag of trail mix will be delicious for you to enjoy and will also be a reminder of all the colors of our Indian tribe. Look for your family's color in the bag. Each color adds to make the bag look especially pretty—just as each one of our family members bring beauty of their own. Enjoy your treat.

*Keeping our ideas centered on our family Indian tribe took some thought. Trail mix was a hit with everyone. There are many varieties, so choose one that your family likes. We bought the mix in bulk and then divided it into colorful cellophane bags and tied the bags with ribbon in the family colors. We also used the family colors by adding M&Ms to the mix in the colors we needed. This made a fun treat and it reminded them of the great time we shared in organizing our family tribe.*

On the THIRD Day of

# Christmas

*We bring to you with love . . .*

**Tribal Sugar Cookies!** We know how much you love sugar cookies, so we have lots of them for you to enjoy today. We had such fun decorating them and trying to make them especially colorful. Be sure to share.

*I knew this was going to be a winner. Everyone likes freshly baked cookies during the holidays, so we were greeted warmly with this one. If you are mailing your gifts, send some cookie cutters and your favorite sugar cookie recipe. You could even include some colored sprinkles and decorations for the cookies.*

While watching our daughter, Julie, make sugar cookies with her little boys, Bowen and Austin, I thought, *We all love these cookies, so there must be a way they can be used for the 12 Days of Christmas.* I got busy looking for cookie cutters pertaining to our Indian tribe theme. I was elated when I found them in local craft stores and in specialty shops.

## Sugar Cookie Recipe

6½ cups flour

2 tsp. baking soda

1 tsp. salt

2 cups sugar

2 eggs

2 tsp. vanilla

1 cup butter

1 cup sour cream

Mix together flour, baking soda, and salt; set aside. Cream together sugar, eggs, vanilla, butter, and sour cream for 2 minutes. Mix all ingredients together and slightly chill. Roll out on lightly floured board and cut into shapes ½-inch thick. Bake at 350 degrees on greased cookie sheet for 10 minutes. Do not brown.

## Sugar Cookie Icing

1 cup shortening

4 cups powdered sugar

⅓ cup evaporated milk

1 tsp. almond flavoring

Mix together well. Add food coloring if desired.

## Cookie on a Stick

Another idea to use with the sugar cookie is to roll a ball of dough about 2 inches thick and then flatten with the bottom of a glass. Place a Popsicle stick inside the dough and bake as per directions. Then ice with the following recipe:

2 egg whites

2 cups powdered sugar

1 tsp. vanilla or almond flavoring

1½ Tbsp. water

Beat egg whites with electric beater until stiff. Gradually add sugar and vanilla. Add water slowly as you beat. Frosting will look like thick enamel paint.

*Spread frosting with a pastry brush or wide watercolor brush. When frosting is completely dry, paint faces on cookie with watercolor brush and food coloring. Use your imagination and make some fun faces of people and animals. Let dry. Wrap each cookie with plastic wrap and tie with ribbon. This was especially successful when we painted Indian faces on them.*

On the FOURTH Day of

# Christmas

*We bring to you with love . . .*

A Christmas Candle! This is a special Christmas candle just for your family. Tonight we want you to light the candle and turn the lights in the room down low while you listen to Mom or Dad read you the very special story we have included.

*Our family enjoys a new holiday candle each year, so we felt sure this was going to be a winner. We found wonderful holiday scents of cinnamon, evergreen, holiday sugar cookies, baked apples, wassail, and many others. Many gift shops carry these, and you will find them in discount stores as well. We had such fun choosing what we thought was the perfect scent for each of our families.*

# The Stolen Holiday

Once upon a time there was a woman—no, a family; no, a village; no, a city; no, a state; no, a country; no, a world—that was upset. They were upset because some very bad things had happened, and they were scared. Not just a bit scared, but Big Time Frightened that the bad things would happen again. Or that different bad things that they could think of would happen—or even new terrible bad things that they haven't even heard of yet and didn't really understand, that those could happen soon. And so they waited and held their breath.

And when it came time for "the holidays," many people said, "Let's not have them this year. What if by having them, we make the bad things happen? What if we let our guard down even for a day and the bad things get us?"

So people began canceling their holidays. They cancelled parties and plane reservations and sending out cards and decorating their homes. They cancelled letters and visits to Grandma and driving to see friends and caroling for sick people in the hospital. They cancelled baking and pageants and feasting and gathering.

They stayed home and waited for the bad things and watched for the bad things and worried all the time. And then, one day, someone asked this question: "If we cancel everything we love, everything we trust and look forward to, haven't the bad things really gotten us anyway? Didn't they win?"

And so one day, that woman, that family, that village, that city, that state, that country, that world all woke up and decided that this was the year not to cancel, but especially to celebrate . . . and they began to hum little holiday songs and leave little holiday surprises around and plan parties and send packages.

But part of what happened was the people started to look at which of the traditions they liked, and they did those All Out. And they thought of the traditions and expectations and demands they Hated and decided that life was too short and precious and uncertain to do those even one more time. And so they didn't. And the phone calls were ever so much sweeter, and the gatherings often ended with hugs and kisses all around the circle. And friends who hadn't talked in years sent each other emails saying, "I miss you. You are still important to me."

And people began volunteering all over the place. Programs had to turn people away because so many people said, "I have so much. I am so grateful. How can I help?"

And they helped in beautiful ways. Miracles happened. People lit candles to remind themselves about how powerful lights are, especially in the darkness. And those lights shone so brightly. And grown-ups spent less time worrying about what they were going to buy their kids and more time creating special memories their children would have for the rest of their lives.

And as the New Year rolled around, a deepest wish was passed from heart to heart for true peace on earth, and that each of us should truly live all the days of our lives.

—PATTI J. CHRISTENSEN

*Since 9/11 our whole world is different; loved ones were lost, buildings crumbled, businesses folded, news became filled with stories of war, and many people retreated in isolation. Truly darkness descended. Yet at the same time, others reached out—hearts and homes opened up as people cared for one another, supported one another, and shared their time, talents, money, and gifts. Surely, light was spread.*

On the FIFTH Day of

# Christmas

*We bring to you with love . . .*

Navajo Tacos! We want you to join us tonight at our home for some delicious Navajo tacos. Doesn't this sound like fun? Wear your Indian headband and we will celebrate our Indian tribe. It will be fun to see all the colors of our tribe while enjoying dinner together. We can hardly wait to see you.

*The holidays are much more special when we get together and share the love of families. It was a fun evening remembering that, once again, there's nothing to compare with the happiness we feel when we are all together. Everyone enjoyed the food and it gave moms a night of relaxation.*

## Navajo Tacos

### Bean Mixture:

3 cups dry beans (soak overnight)

1 lbs. ground chuck

1 chopped onion

3 Tbsp. chili powder

2 cloves minced garlic

3 Tbsp. flour

Cook beans for three hours or until soft; add some salt. Brown ground chuck, onion, chili powder, and garlic together. Add flour when meat is done. Let it brown and then add to beans. Add salt, pepper, and chili powder to taste.

### Scones:

½ tsp. yeast

2¼ cups warm water, divided

2 cups warm water

¼ cup melted butter

1 cup sugar

3 cups flour

½ Tbsp. salt

½ tsp. soda

½ Tbsp. baking powder

Mix yeast and ¼ cup warm water and set aside. In separate bowl, mix remaining 2 cups warm water, melted butter, and sugar. Add flour and let rise until doubled. Stir down and add remaining ingredients. Add more flour until no longer sticky. Divide dough into 3-inch pieces. Pat back and forth and pull until flat and round. Fry each side of scone in vegetable oil until golden brown. Dough will keep in the refrigerator for approximately two weeks.

✳*Top with bean mixture, diced tomatoes, shredded lettuce, sliced olives, sour cream, salsa, and cheese.*

On the SIXTH Day of

# Christmas

*We bring to you with love . . .*

Hoot Nanny Pancakes! Remember how much we all love these yummy pancakes. Since today is Saturday and everyone should be home, we are inviting you all to come to our home this morning for Hoot Nanny Pancakes. We will have such a wonderful time together, and you can eat all the pancakes your tummies will hold. Remember what you have to say when the pancakes come out of the oven.

*Martie McLean shared this recipe with me. I cling to every word she says because it is either so profound that I never want to forget it or so funny that I can't forget it! So it was with the Hoot Nanny Pancakes. She had several ladies over for a brunch one morning and informed us that as she brought the pancakes out of the oven, we were to say, "Hoot Nanny, Hoot Nanny, Hoot, Hoot, Hoot!" Martie said this was necessary to make the pancakes turn out just right.*

We use this with our Indian theme also. It's so fun and quite a sight when the grandchildren wear their Indian headdresses. Children love to participate in preparing the meal in any way they can—but especially if it involves saying the Hoot Nanny chant.

## Hoot Nanny Pancakes

6 eggs
1 cup flour
½ cup butter
1 cup whole milk
½ tsp. salt

Preheat oven to 425 degrees. Melt butter in 9 x 13 baking pan until bubbly. Whip eggs and milk together. Sift in flour and salt. Pour batter into pan over melted butter. Bake 20 to 25 minutes.

*Serve with warm syrup or jam.*

On the SEVENTH Day of

## Christmas

We bring to you with love . . .

A Christmas Story! We are providing a Christmas story for Mom and Dad to read to you tonight. Perhaps you could all sit "Indian style" as you listen. This will help remind you of our family Indian tribe and how special each member of the tribe is. Talk about the true meaning of Christmas and how blessed we are to know of the Christ child's birth. We love you so much.

*There are many wonderful Christmas stories that you can share with your family. We included a story in our 12 Days of Christmas and asked the parents to gather their families together as they read the beautiful story. It brings families closer together as they share stories about the true meaning of Christmas. This is an especially easy one to mail.*

## Spirit of Christmas

'Twas the first night of Christmas, a long time ago,
The hillside was peaceful, the moon was aglow.
The world couldn't know from what happened before,
That men would remember this night evermore.
The sheep on the hillside, the day's journey over,
Were dreaming sweet dreams of a field full of clover.
The shepherds were watchful while guarding their flock.
The earth was their pillow; the stars were their clock.
Then all of a sudden they jumped at the sight,
Of the sky all ablaze with a heavenly light.
They huddled in fear, then they started to rise,
As the lightening-like flash tore open the skies.
The heavens were split by the silvery ray.
The dark disappeared and the night became day.
And lo, at the end of the rainbow of light,
Appeared then an angel to banish their fright.
The angel brought news of a birth in a manger,
And bade them to hasten to welcome the stranger.
For Mary had just given birth to a boy,
Whose coming would bring so much comfort and joy.
A choir of angels looked down from the sky,
And heavenly voices were heard from on high.
Peace be on earth and good will to all men.
The Savior has come on this night. Amen.
The heavenly angels then faded from sight,
The sky once again turned from day into night.
The shepherds all quietly rose from the ground,
And hurried to go where the child would be found.
As they reached Bethlehem and the inn was in sight,
From the barn came a trickle or half-hidden light.
It led like a path to a soft little bed,
And shone very tenderly on the child's head.
The child in the manger was sleeping so sound,
His eyes were still closed as the shepherds stood around.
From that instance of grace, on that night long ago,
Thousands of years would be warmed by the glow.

Guided by light from a bright shining star
Came a pilgrimage led of three kings from afar.
They were dressed in the finest of satin and lace,
Their complexions were that of an Orient race.
The three wealthy kings were wise men and proud,
But they went to the Christ child and solemnly bowed.
They came bearing treasures of incense and gold,
To that sweet little child, still not very old.
The star in the sky twinkled down from above,
The world was awakened to kindness and love.
The past was forgotten, the future was brought,
And the Spirit of Christmas was born on that night.

—Anonymous

On the EIGHTH Day of

Christmas

We bring to you with love . . .

Glow-in-the-Dark Necklaces and Bracelets!
This new jewelry is especially fun! Turn out the lights
tonight while you sing some Christmas carols and see
the glow of your necklaces and bracelets.

*You can find these at your local dollar store or online catalog com-*
*panies that feature trinkets and inexpensive toys. There always seems*
*to be something that fits our theme and is quite inexpensive: inter-*
*twined bouncing balls with all the colors of our family tribe or school*
*pencils engraved with the name of our Indian tribe—anything to*
*remind them that they are a part of a family who loves them.*

On the NINTH Day of

# Christmas

*We bring to you with love . .*

Handmade Greeting Cards! We have had such fun making these greeting cards for your family. They can be used throughout the year to send special greetings to your family and friends. We have included some supplies for you to try making some. It's fun!

*You can find everything you will need at any specialty shop that carries scrapbook supplies. We made twelve cards for each family—in their family's tribal color, of course. "Thank You," "Thinking of You," "Happy Birthday," "Get Well Soon," and "Congratulations" were some of the ideas we used. When you visit the scrapbook store, check out the samples on display: they'll give you great ideas for making your own cards. These are easy to mail and can be made ahead of time.*

On the TENTH Day of

# Christmas

*We bring to you with love . . .*

Christmas Plum Pudding! This is a special treat for your family tonight. Plum pudding isn't made very often, but we treasure a recipe that has been in our family for years. Plum pudding brings special memories of years past. We hope it will do the same for you.

*It's hard to find a good plum pudding recipe, so I have treasured this one through the years. It was a special dessert for each family, and they remembered having this each Christmas as they were growing up. This was a gift we had to deliver on the day we had chosen, but if you are mailing your gifts, you might consider sending the recipe along with a holiday pan for making the pudding.*

# Christmas Plum Pudding

| | |
|---|---|
| 4 slices bread | 2 cups raisins |
| 1 cup milk | 1 cup chopped dates |
| 1 cup flour | ½ cup broken walnuts |
| 1 tsp. baking soda | 2 slightly beaten eggs |
| ½ tsp. salt | 6 oz. (2 cups) beef suet |
| 2 tsp. cinnamon | 1 cup brown sugar |
| 1 tsp. cloves | ¼ cup orange juice |
| 1 tsp. mace | 1 tsp. vanilla |

Tear bread slices into pieces. Soak torn bread pieces in milk; use a fork to break up well. Sift together flour, baking soda, salt, cinnamon, cloves, and mace; add raisins, chopped dates, and broken walnuts. Mix well. Add finely chopped beef suet, brown sugar, orange juice, and vanilla to bread mixture. Stir bread-suet mixture into flour mixture. Pour into greased 2-quart mold; cover with aluminum foil and tie securely with string. Place on rack in deep kettle; pour in 1 inch of boiling water and put lid on kettle. Steam 3½ hours, adding more water when needed. Cool about 10 minutes before taking pudding out of mold. Garnish with red candied cherries and serve warm with sauce.

### Fluffy Hard Sauce:
½ cup butter
1 tsp. vanilla
2 cups powdered sugar
1 stiffly beaten egg white

Cream together butter and vanilla. Gradually add sifted powdered sugar. Cream together until fluffy. Fold in egg white. Serves 12.

✳*After steaming the pudding in an attractive mold and then letting it cool, we wrapped it in red or green cellophane and tied it with Christmas ribbon.*

On the ELEVENTH Day of

# Christmas

*We bring to you with love . . .*

**Hot Dog & Marshmallow Sticks!** Now when we get together for roasting marshmallows and hot dogs, you can use sticks in your family's tribal color. No more searching for a stick! We have such wonderful memories of the times we have spent 'round the fire with you. Let's make lots more memories.

*I was fortunate to find sturdy hot dog sticks in just the right family tribal colors at a nearby Christmas boutique. We always had a hard time gathering enough roasting sticks, so these were perfect. They are 3-foot copper sticks with 6-inch round wooden handles. They had holes drilled through the end of the handle and a colorful piece of cording tied through the hole so they could be hung up when not in use. Everyone loved these, and we made plans to use them right away.*

On the TWELFTH Day of

# Christmas

*We bring to you with love . .*

Old-Fashioned Candy Sticks! Here are some delicious candy sticks for you to enjoy today. This candy reminded us of the candy we used to enjoy when we were young children like you. Can you believe we found them in the colors of our Indian tribe? We were excited to buy them for you. Think of how much we love you while you enjoy your candy.

*The grandchildren enjoyed the day they received candy sticks in the flavors that matched the tribal colors of each family. I bought enough for each family to have plenty.*

# Chapter Eight

## *The Polar Express*

*"Christmas, my child, is love in action. Every time we love, each time we give, it's Christmas."*

—Dale Evans Rogers

Our grandchildren love *The Polar Express* book, music, and movie. One little grandson Adam learned the words to one of the songs at age three and could sing it beautifully. What a touching moment for grandparents. We plan to make it a theme for the 12 Days of Christmas in the near future. I'll share some of the ideas I have gathered.

On the FIRST Day of

*Christmas*

*We bring to you with love . . .*

The Polar Express Book! (By Chris Van Allsburg)
What a fabulous book! We read this book and knew we
wanted each family to have their own copy. We hope
you will enjoy reading it together tonight as a family
and then start looking forward to your "Polar Express"
adventure this holiday season. We can hardly wait to
share this with you!

*Each family will want a copy for their collection. Give it early so they
can read the story and relate it to their other gifts. The book can be
purchased at most bookstores, and often you can get a bell with the
book.*

On the SECOND Day of

*Christmas*

*We bring to you with love . . .*

Bell from the Polar Express! Who doesn't want a bell from Santa's sleigh? The bell is a symbol of the true spirit of Christmas. It lies in your heart. Listen . . . can you hear the bell? "Believers" can hear the sound of the bell, and it encourages them to do good deeds to others and to feel the true spirit of Christmas. Children, listen for the sweet sound of the bell this Christmas.

*You can find these small bells at most craft stores or buy it with the book at most bookstores. They usually come with a long ribbon or cord so the children can wear them around their necks.*

On the THIRD Day of

# Christmas

*We bring to you with love . . .*

Christmas Pajamas! The little boy in the Polar Express story wears his PJs and a bathrobe, so we thought you might enjoy having one of your own. You'll look adorable!

*The little ones would love some new winter pajamas to go along with this theme. You might want to give a bathrobe instead of—or along with—the pajamas.*

On the FOURTH Day of

Christmas

*We bring to you with love . . .*

Reindeer Craft! We hope you enjoy making this craft with your family. If you need help, ask Mom, Dad, or an older brother or sister. Have fun being creative, and make sure to munch on these cookies we have included while you're working!

*Give each member of the family material to make a reindeer. You can include everything they will need. This will be a great activity for everyone to participate in. Oh, and you may want to bake them some reindeer-shaped cookies to enjoy while they make their craft. They will have lots of fun.*

# Reindeer Craft

4 Popsicle sticks
2 goggle eyes
2 brown pipe cleaners
1 small, red pom-pom
8 inches yarn (any color)
glue

*Face:* Glue Popsicle sticks together to form a triangle with the point facing down.

*Eyes:* Glue the eyes on each of the two top corners.

*Antlers:* Wrap the pipe cleaners around the top Popsicle stick and shape like antlers.

*Nose:* Glue the red pom-pom nose to the Popsicle stick at the bottom point of the triangle.

*Hanger:* Tie yarn around the top stick to make a hanger for the decoration to hang from.

On the FIFTH Day of

# Christmas

*We bring to you with love...*

**Tickets to Ride the Polar Express Train!** Here are some tickets for your family to ride on a real Polar Express train! Buckle up for and snuggle in for the ride. They even serve hot chocolate—just like in the movie.

*We learned about a Polar Express train in our area that is available for rides during the holiday season. Now wouldn't children love this . . . a ride on the Polar Express! This could be the highlight of the 12 Days of Christmas by taking all the children for a wonderful day together riding the Polar Express. Start checking your local newspapers early for information. Such precious memories will be made—so don't forget to take along your camera.*

On the SIXTH Day of

# Christmas

*We bring to you with love . . .*

Train- and Bell-Shaped Lollipops! Here are some yummy lollipops for you to enjoy. We all love chocolate, so you are sure to eat these up quickly. Have fun! We love you so much.

*During the holiday season these should be easy to find in specialty shops or craft stores. Consider making the homemade lollipops again (see page 11). They are easy to make and fun to do. Look for molds to go with this theme, and give the children lots of colors and flavors.*

On the SEVENTH Day of

# Christmas

*We bring to you with love . . .*

An Evening with Grandma and Grandpa! Here is a ticket for one special evening with NeNa and PaPa on our own Polar Express train. Make sure to dress comfy in your Christmas pajamas! We'll be reading *The Polar Express,* sipping on hot chocolate, and munching on donuts.

*Send the "ticket" out a few days early so they can reserve the date. When they arrive, you (the conductor) could greet them and punch their ticket. Wouldn't it be fun if you could find a conductor's hat? Set up the room with rows of chairs as if on a train. Talk with the children about the true meaning of Christmas and how important it is to "believe." Any opportunity to reinforce this with our children and grandchildren is always a good thing!*

On the EIGHTH Day of

# Christmas

*We bring to you with love . . .*

**Polar Express Mugs!** How fun is it to have your very own Polar Express mug? We have personalized each mug so you won't get them mixed up. We know how you love hot chocolate, so be sure to use your new mug each time you celebrate our theme.

*You will find wonderful Christmas mugs in discount stores and in specialty shops. One suggestion is to purchase solid colored mugs and paint a message from the Polar Express on the mug, such as "Believe" or "The Polar Express." I have seen mugs with the printing already on them; these could easily be found on the Internet.*

On the NINTH Day of

# Christmas

*We bring to you with love . . .*

A Christmas Pillow! We hope this pillow will find a special place in your home this year. When you read the message "Just Believe," we hope you will remember the little boy in the Polar Express story and how his Christmas adventure reminded him of how important it is to always believe. We never get too old to believe. We believe in each one of you and love you so much.

*Create or buy a beautiful Christmas pillows to display on a shelf or a couch. You could stitch the word "Believe" on muslin and then sew pretty Christmas fabric around the muslin, with a matching piece for the back. Stuff the pillow with fiberfill or a pillow form. Let it serve as a reminder of your theme during the holidays. You should also be able to find pillows available in some craft boutiques and shops—so start looking early!*

On the TENTH Day of

# Christmas

*We bring to you with love . . .*

**"Believe" Sign!** We loved this sign and wanted to make sure each of our special families have this reminder in their homes to believe. We do believe, don't we? How blessed we are as a family to know how crucial it is to believe in the really important things in life.

*If you are crafty, make a small, wooden sign that fits on an easel and can be displayed in the home. The word "Believe" would be perfect or use the phrase said by the conductor: "Seeing is believing, but sometimes the most real things in the world are the things we can't see." This sign will serve as a reminder of the importance of believing in the true meaning of Christmas.*

This too is something you should be able to find at some of the holiday boutiques, or you could order one to be made for you there. I am usually able to find things that are a little more unique at holiday boutiques. If you choose to make it yourself, purchase your wood, cut it to size, sand it so it will be smooth and ready to paint in the color of your choice. You can choose to either purchase the words that are already cut from vinyl or you can stencil the words on the wood yourself. Again, the Internet is a wonderful source of information for making these signs. I chose to distress the sign on the edges with my sander, and then I sprayed it with a lacquer spray so it had a nice finished look. Also consider stitching the words on a piece of fabric and then use attractive nail heads to hold the fabric on the board you have prepared. Fraying the ends of the fabric makes it especially attractive.

On the ELEVENTH Day of

# Christmas

*We bring to you with love . . .*

The Polar Express Movie! We're going to have a great time together tonight. We will pick you up at seven o'clock sharp to take you to see *The Polar Express* movie. Don't worry, we'll have you home early so you can still spend time with your family!

*Check around to see where* The Polar Express *movie is playing in your area and treat the children to a movie! It could be a wonderful outing, perhaps followed with—what else?—a cup of hot chocolate! You could also add this DVD to their collection of holiday movies.*

On the TWELFTH Day of

# Christmas

*We bring to you with love . . .*

A Christmas Bell of Service! Do an act of service in secret for a neighbor or friend and leave this little bell on their doorstep along with a message from *The Polar Express*. Maybe some homemade cookies or bread would bring a big smile to their faces.

*Suggest to your family that they do an act of service in secret and leave a small bell along, with a thought from the story of the Polar Express, on the doorstep of the family for whom they performed the service. This will bring the story to more families and they too will enjoy listening for the ringing of the bell for all believers.*

# Chapter Nine

*Give as the Savior Gave*

*"As a small boy on the farm during the heat of the summer, I remember my grandmother, Mary Finlinson, cooking our delicious meals on a hot wood stove. When the wood box next to the stove became empty, Grandmother silently picked it up, refilled it from the pile of cedar wood outside, and brought the heavily laden box back into the house. I was so interested in the conversation in the kitchen that I sat there and let my beloved grandmother refill the kitchen wood box. I feel ashamed of myself and have regretted my omission all my life. I hope someday to ask for her forgiveness."*

—James E. Faust

Developing this theme will be satisfying to both you and your family. What better example is there to follow than that of the Savior, Jesus Christ? He taught us how to live by his example. Some of the gifts you receive this year will be centered around family preparedness. Our world has seen many tragedies in the past few years, and we need to prepare for future happenings to avoid pain and loss should a disaster occur. Ignorance is not bliss!

As parents and grandparents, we want to make sure our families have the necessary things they will need to sustain them until help can arrive. Check with your local bookstores and look on the Internet for information on family preparedness. There are many sources we can turn to for the information we need.

On the FIRST Day of

# Christmas

*We bring to you with love . . .*

A First Aid Kit! The Savior healed the sick—and now with this first aid kit, you can too. We included items needed in times of disaster. Go through the kit together and discuss how each item can help you. We have also included some hard candy as a little treat to keep in your kit. Here's a list of the items inside:

| | | |
|---|---|---|
| sterile gauze | antibiotic cream | tweezers |
| adhesive tape | antiseptic solution | sharp scissors |
| elastic bandages | aspirin | safety pins |
| antiseptic wipes | cough drops | cold packs |
| soap | ibuprofen | first-aid manual |

*You can find first aid kits in most sports stores and local retail stores, but we found an Internet site that allowed us to buy items at wholesale prices, and they had everything we wanted for our kits. Each family can customize their kits to suit their family. There are all kinds of containers to choose from, but keep in mind that it needs to be light-weight, have handles, and be big enough to fit everything inside. Plastic tackle boxes or containers for storing art supplies are ideal.*

On the SECOND Day of

# Christmas

*We bring to you with love . . .*

Food Storage! The Savior fed the hungry; now with this food storage, you can be assured that you will never go hungry, even in very hard times. Here are some foods that preserve well and could help you from going hungry: canned tuna and chicken, mayonnaise, beans, rice, salt, sugar, pancake mix, syrup, crackers, peanut butter, jelly, and bottles of water. Please talk as a family and make plans to add to your food storage. Everyone in the family can be involved in this project.

*There would be nothing worse than knowing our family was without food during a time of disaster. This is only a beginning, but we wanted them to have enough food to sustain life until help arrives. You can also put together 72-hour kits or purchase them via the Internet. There are instructions available for these on the Internet or in local bookstores.*

## When I Feel His Love

Quiet times of revelation tune my heart to see
Tender mercies of the Lord are daily shown to me.
As I feel the love of God I seem to understand
I can be an instrument in Heavenly Father's hands.
And when I feel His love, my heart has one desire—
To share the joy and warmth His perfect love inspires.
My hands reach out to all in purest charity
That other souls may feel His love through me.

Quiet times of inspiration touch me and I feel
God's pure love is guiding me, and His promises are real.
As I nurture those I love within my daily sphere,
I feel strength beyond my own and know that God is near.
And when I feel His love, my heart has one desire:
To share the joy and warmth His perfect love inspires.
My hands reach out to all in purest charity
That other souls may feel His love through me.

—JANICE KAPP PERRY

On the THIRD Day of

# Christmas

*We bring to you with love . . .*

A Mirror! The Savior gave sight to the blind. The beautiful mirror we are giving you today will help to remind you that Jesus sees all the good things about us, so always try to do the things that are right. Remember to always follow the Savior's example.

*Pick out a mirror that will match nicely in their home. On the mirror, you could either etch or paint, "Do You See What I See?" This can be a daily reminder to keep our lives clean and pure. Etching kits can be purchased in craft stores and aren't difficult to use.*

On the FOURTH Day of

# Christmas

*We bring to you with love . . .*

A Service Project! The Savior caused the lame to walk; as our service project this year we will help those less fortunate than ourselves. Many children do not have warm shoes for winter. A local radio station in our town collects money at Christmas to buy shoes for needy children. Let's contribute to that cause and help provide shoes for some special children. The Savior provided miracles, and we can provide miracles in our own way. Let's empty our piggy banks and help buy shoes for those in need.

*Check with your local radio stations to see if they offer this. What a great cause! Another suggestion would be to purchase shoes for families you know are in need and leave them on their doorstep. Often churches collect items to be given out at Christmas, so you may also want to consider donating that way.*

On the FIFTH Day of

# Christmas

*We bring to you with love . . .*

A Serenity Rock Fountain! The Savior calmed the seas; this fountain has a very calming effect and will bring hours of relaxation not only during the hustle and bustle of the holidays but for the rest of the year too.

*Taking time for ourselves is important. We wanted to encourage some time for relaxation. You could also include an emergency Stress Relief Kit! Instructions for making your own Stress Relief Kit are included on the following page.*

## Chocolate Kisses
To remind you how much you are loved.

## Fire Starter
To light your fire when you feel burned out.

## Tootsie Rolls
To remind you not to bite off more than you can chew.

## Smarties
To help you on those days when you don't feel so smart.

## Starbursts
To give you that burst of energy when there doesn't seem to be any.

## Snickers
To remind you to take time to laugh.

## a Bag
To help you keep it all together and to give you food for thought.

## a Candle
To remind you that you can brighten someone's day!

*Fountains can be found in your local department stores or discount stores. The price is approximately twenty-five dollars for an average size fountain.*

On the SIXTH Day of

*Christmas*

*We bring to you with love . . .*

An Ornament to Remind You of Christ! The Savior gave his life for us. Christ's greatest gift of all is the Atonement. Only he could love us enough to give his very life for us. We have the promise of eternal life because of his great sacrifice. Take time to reflect on the importance of the Atonement in our lives and talk about what we can do to show our love for our Savior.

*Your gift today is an ornament for their memory tree. Let them know that it serves to remind them of his unconditional love. Tie a crimson ribbon around the head of a nail and attach the verse on the following page.*

## It's Christmas at Our House

It's Christmas at our house,
And we're putting up the tree.
I wish I could find one simple way
To remember Christ's gift to me.
Some little sign or symbol
To show friends stopping by
The little babe was born one day,
But he really came to die.
Some symbol of his nail-pierced hands—
The blood he shed for me.
What if I hung a simple nail
Upon my Christmas tree.
A crimson bow tied round the nail
As his blood flowed down so free
To save each person from their sins,
And redeem us for eternity.
I know it was His love for us
That held him to that tree.
But when I see that simple nail
I know he died for me.

—ANONYMOUS

*Print or hand-write this verse on white card stock and cut card stock to appropriate size to fit with the nail. Attach to the nail by punching a hole through the top and inserting the red ribbon through the nail. Then tie the ribbon around the nail.*

On the SEVENTH Day of

# Christmas

*We bring to you with love . . .*

A Christmas Book! The Savior gave hope to a troubled world; add this wonderful book entitled *The Peace Giver: How Christ Offers to Heal Our Hearts and Homes* (by James L. Ferrell) to your collection of Christmas books. Let's enjoy reading this book and sharing ideas and thoughts together.

*You could include a puzzle for the children to enjoy while the parents read their new book.*

In *The Peace Giver*, a couple struggles with pain and loneliness as their marriage disintegrates into hurtful words and actions that push them further apart. As they learn the true power and mercy of the Atonement, their hearts are slowly softened. *The Peace Giver* can be purchased at your local bookstore.

On the EIGHTH Day of

# Christmas

*We bring to you with love . . .*

The Christmas Star of Service! The Savior gave us examples of service; we were excited about giving this small wooden star to you. Read the poem we have included to learn the meaning behind "The Christmas Star of Service"!

*Our star was given the name of "The Christmas Star of Service." Read the following poem and it will tell exactly what they need to do.*

## The Christmas Star

Here's a magical Christmas Star
With a tradition old and true.
May it bring you warmth and love
Not only at Christmas, but all year through.
Now every day 'till the New Year
Find someone in your home,
And secretly do a deed of love
So your identity won't be known.
And when the secret act is done,
Place the star upon their bed.
They in turn do a secret deed
For another, it is said.
And like the star so long ago
Lit the sky for all the world to see,
May this star bring light and joy
To your wonderful family.

—ANONYMOUS

## Christmas Star of Service

*Cut out wooden stars about 6 inches tall and spray them with gold paint.

*Drill a hole in the bottom of the star and glue in a wooden dowel so it can easily be held.

*Tie colorful streamers to the dowel to make it more fun for the children.

Our children commented that this was a great way of encouraging their family to serve one another. They would make a bed, pick up some toys, or do a chore that had been assigned to a brother or sister and then leave the star on that person's pillow. Parents can also be involved in this and show, through their example, the many acts of service we can perform for family members.

On the NINTH Day of

Christmas

*We bring to you with love . . .*

A Service Visit! The Savior helped the needy; tonight we will share a special experience together. We will be going to visit a homeless shelter. We will see and appreciate how blessed we are in our families to have the necessities and luxuries that we enjoy daily. We will also have the opportunity to see how thankful the homeless are for the food that we can provide for them.

*Perhaps they could meet at your home and caravan together to the shelter. After visiting the homeless shelter, you could suggest your family return to your home for a treat. This recipe for Poor Man's Pie seemed to fit right in.*

# Poor Man's Pie

1 cup flour
1 cup milk
1 cup sugar
1 tsp. salt
1 tsp. baking powder
½ cup melted butter

Mix above ingredients together. Pour into 9 x 13 baking pan. Spoon any fruit pie filling on top of mixture. Bake at 350 degrees until brown.

*Delicious served with whipped cream or ice cream.*

On the TENTH Day of

# Christmas

*We bring to you with love . . .*

A Fleece Blanket! The Savior gave comfort; one of the things we tend to think of when we think of comfort is a warm blanket. Wrap the blanket around yourself and remember how much the Savior loves you. He loves to bring us comfort in times of need. We hope you will always find comfort in his love.

*Fleece blankets are easy to make, and there are prints of all kinds available. Directions to make a fleece blanket are included on the following page.*

## Fleece Blanket

❋Determine what size blanket you want to make. For a child's blanket, use a 45-inch wide piece of cloth; for an adult, a 60-inch. Heavyweight polar fleece is usually best.

❋Even out the cut edges of the fabric, if necessary. Lay out your fabric wrong side up on a cutting board and use the board's measuring guidelines to determine whether the edges are straight.

❋Trim the cut edges of the fabric so they are even. If you do not want fringe on your blanket, you are finished.

**Fringe:**

❋Lay your blanket out horizontally in front of you, wrong side up.

❋Use a fabric cutting board, a yardstick, and a fabric marking pen to draw a vertical line at each end of your blanket. Each line should be 6 inches from each cut edge.

❋Draw a series of horizontal lines, ½ inch apart, between each vertical line drawn in the previous step and each cut edge.

❋Use a pair of dressmaker shears or a rotary cutter to cut along each of the horizontal lines made in the previous step. This makes the fringe for your blanket.

❋Tie a knot at the top of each piece of fringe to give it a finished look.

On the ELEVENTH Day of
*Christmas*
*We bring to you with love . . .*

A Prayer Plant! The Savior taught us how to pray; there are many examples throughout the scriptures of the Apostles and prophets turning to our Heavenly Father in prayer. The Savior prayed to our Heavenly Father and taught us by example how important this is in our lives. We need to remember to pray every day and share with him both the happy and sad times. He is our friend and he loves us. He will always be there to help us through our trials. We hope you will always feel of his love and of our love.

*"Prayer Plants" are beautiful plants known for their ability to close their leaves at night, which gives them their name. When they see these little leaves closing, it can be a reminder that we need to always close our day with prayer. Include instructions for caring for their plant—just as our Heavenly Father gave us instructions for our personal care and growth.*

Prayer Plants are available as small starter plants in 3- and 4-inch containers as well as 6-inch pots and trellises, along with 6- and 8-inch hanging baskets. The plant is a low growing plant, usually not more than 12 inches in height or 20 inches in width. You should be able to find these plants at your local nursery.

## I'm Trying To Be like Jesus

I'm trying to be like Jesus;
I'm following in his ways.
I'm trying to love as he did,
In all that I do and say.
At times I am tempted to make a wrong choice,
But I try to listen as the still small voice whispers,

"Love one another as Jesus loves you.
Try to show kindness in all that you do.
Be gentle and loving in deed and in thought,
For these are the things Jesus taught."

I'm trying to love my neighbor;
I'm learning to serve my friends.
I watch for the day of gladness
When Jesus will come again.
I try to remember the lessons he taught.
Then the Holy Spirit enters into my thoughts, saying:

"Love one another as Jesus loves you
Try to show kindness in all that you do,
Be gentle and loving in deed and in thought
For these are the things I'm taught."

—JANICE KAPP PERRY

*Copyright 1980. Used with permission

On the TWELFTH Day of

# Christmas

*We bring to you with love . . .*

A Forgiveness Basket! The Savior taught us how to forgive; we often harbor bad feelings toward another person, and we don't know how to let go of these feelings. Tonight you can throw those bad feelings away. Build a big fire in your fire pit or fireplace and hold a ceremony where each one of you throws a pinecone into the fire. The pinecone will represent the bad feelings you may have toward another person. We have been taught how important it is to forgive those who may have offended us in some way—let's learn to forgive as the Savior taught us when he was here on earth.

*Put enough pinecones in a basket so that each member of the family can have one. Decorate the basket with a pretty Christmas ribbon.*

# Conclusion

*Your Reward—It's Worth the Effort*

*"Traditions . . . keep us close to the great heritage which is ours. . . . If we will build righteous traditions in our families, the light of the gospel can grow ever brighter in [our] lives . . . we can look forward to that glorious day when we will all be united together as eternal family units to reap the everlasting joy promised by our Eternal Father for His righteous children."*

—L. Tom Perry

I give thanks to a loving Father in Heaven who listened to a mother praying for help in making Christmas what it could be in our home. Yes, the change had to begin with me because he had planted that desire and need in my heart. How grateful I am for the sweet experiences the 12 Days of Christmas have allowed our family. Love has grown within our family for one another. Has the spirit of the 12 Days of Christmas spread beyond Sterling and me? Well, as they say, the proof is in the pudding. We knew our message of love had been received and understood when our children returned a special gift of love to us. This is the joy Sterling and I experienced last Christmas.

It began on the evening of December 14th. Our doorbell rang, and we could hear the voices of carolers on our front steps. We hurried to the door expecting to see a few familiar faces from our neighborhood, but, instead, we were greeted with voices and faces that we knew and loved— our children and grandchildren. What a wonderful surprise! When they had finished singing, they handed us a letter and asked that I read it aloud. They just can't learn that Mom is much too emotional for this. Nevertheless, I read, with tears streaming down my face, the following letter from our children and grandchildren:

Dear Mom and Dad,

For the past six years we have felt the excitement, the spirit, and the love of the 12 Days of Christmas. We want you to know how much we appreciate all the hard work: all the countless hours of thought and prayer spent deciding what theme you should follow and all the time put into twelve wonderful days of Christmas. You both have helped bring the true meaning of Christmas into each of our homes. You have brought our families together during the hustle and bustle of the season. Thank you for that. Well, we want to be just like you. This year we bring to you both your very own 12 Days of Christmas—but with a twist! We want to change it a bit and call it . . . *the 12 "Dates" of Christmas.*

We are excited this year to give back to you what you have given to us these past years. You will now get to experience what we feel for twelve days. We have been blessed to have lived in a home where we learned firsthand how a mother and father should treat one another and how they should love one another. We remember watching you two holding hands while shopping, wanting to always spend time together, and serving others together. You seemed to always be "side by side, hand in hand, and heart to heart." The reason we chose "dates" instead of "days" is because we know the value of your eternal marriage and we know how much you two love being together. We love you both so much. Thank you for being so good to us, for loving us and our children, and—most important—for loving each other. Merry Christmas, Mom and Dad!

Love,
*Your Children*

Our children then presented us with the first "date" of Christmas, which was lunch and a movie. The following dates were filled with concert tickets, breakfast at a lovely restaurant, gift certificates for shopping at our local mall, dinner at our favorite restaurant, a matching tie and blouse, an ornament for our memory tree, a DVD and movie treats, a book put together especially for us, a wall hanging of our family tree, and, yes, a day of service. What could we say to that? It was an unforgettable experience for Sterling and me. But even more important, the fact that our children had caught the vision of the 12 Days of Christmas and had the desire to share that vision was touching beyond words.

So to conclude, let's go back to the statement, "Give good and happy memories to your children . . . not pampering or overindulging, not satisfying everything they take a fancy to—but memories of love, encouragement, of peace and harmony and happiness at home—memories that will bless and lift their lives wherever they are, always and forever." My heart tells me we have found a more meaningful way to celebrate Christmas in our family. The response from our children and grandchildren has been a testimony to us that we are doing something right.

What memories have we given our children? Will they remember the times we became upset with their childhood messes, or will they remember the many hours spent making the 12 Days of Christmas special and meaningful for them? We pray with all our hearts that they know and believe that they are the most important people in our lives and providing a more meaningful Christmas for them is our yearly goal.

One son-in-law shared with us how busy his family is and how it is difficult to find time during the busy holidays to do the things that are most important. He expressed his gratitude to us for allowing his family time to come together each day, if only for a short while, and express their love for one another and for their Savior during the 12 Days of Christmas. He felt this was a true blessing in their lives and hopes we continue the tradition.

We have the same concerns for our family that you have for yours. Our greatest desire is that each of them will become loving individuals who are willing to share their love with others. Do you see now that we *can* give a more meaningful Christmas to those we love? With our hearts involved, we know we can succeed. Your reward for your effort will be worth every minute you have given in service to your family.

It is our hope that some of the ideas shared here will light a spark in your heart for a new way to express your love to your family. In a troubled world, we never want there to be a doubt of any kind when it comes to *love*.

# About the Author

Betty LaFon Van Orden was born in Cambria, Virginia. She attended Brigham Young University and majored in psychology.

Betty is a member of The Church of Jesus Christ of Latter-day Saints and has served in many auxiliaries. Betty has also served on various committees in her community, helping to improve the guidelines and standards that govern the activities of high school students.

Betty and her husband, Sterling, are presently living in Syracuse, Utah. They are service missionaries in Salt Lake City at the Conference Center. They have six children and twenty grandchildren.